EX LIBRIS

IKIGAI

The Japanese Secret to a Long and Happy Life

HÉCTOR GARCÍA

AND

FRANCESC MIRALLES

Translated by Heather Cleary

HUTCHINSON
LONDON

Hutchinson
20 Vauxhall Bridge Road
London SW1V 2SA

Hutchinson is part of the Penguin Random House group of companies
whose addresses can be found at global.penguinrandomhouse.com

Penguin
Random House
UK

158.1

Originally published in Spanish as *Ikigai: Los secretos de Japón
para una vida larga y feliz* by Ediciones Urano in 2016
First published in the US by Penguin Books in 2017
First published in the United Kingdom by Hutchinson in 2017

www.penguin.co.uk

A CIP catalogue record for this book is available from the British Library.

ISBN 9781786330895

Typeset in Arno Pro by Katy Riegel, USA
Printed and bound in Great Britain by Clays Ltd, St Ives plc

For my brother, Aitor,
who's said to me more often than anyone else,
"I don't know what to do with my life."
—HÉCTOR GARCÍA

For all my past, present, and future friends,
for being my home and my motivation along
the way.
—FRANCESC MIRALLES

Only staying active will make you want to live a hundred years.

—Japanese proverb

CONTENTS

IKIGAI

Ikigai: A mysterious word

THIS BOOK FIRST came into being on a rainy night in Tokyo, when its authors sat down together for the first time in one of the city's tiny bars.

We had read each other's work but had never met, thanks to the thousands of miles that separate Barcelona from the capital of Japan. Then a mutual acquaintance put us in touch, launching a friendship that led to this project and seems destined to last a lifetime.

The next time we got together, a year later, we strolled through a park in downtown Tokyo and ended up talking about trends in Western psychology, specifically logotherapy, which helps people find their purpose in life.

We remarked that Viktor Frankl's logotherapy had gone

out of fashion among practicing therapists, who favored other schools of psychology, though people still search for meaning in what they do and how they live. We ask ourselves things like:

What is the meaning of my life?

Is the point just to live longer, or should I seek a higher purpose?

Why do some people know what they want and have a passion for life, while others languish in confusion?

At some point in our conversation, the mysterious word *ikigai* came up.

This Japanese concept, which translates roughly as "the happiness of always being busy," is like logotherapy, but it goes a step beyond. It also seems to be one way of explaining the extraordinary longevity of the Japanese, especially on the island of Okinawa, where there are 24.55 people over the age of 100 for every 100,000 inhabitants—far more than the global average.

Those who study why the inhabitants of this island in the south of Japan live longer than people anywhere else in the world believe that one of the keys—in addition to a healthful diet, a simple life in the outdoors, green tea, and the subtropical climate (its average temperature is like that of Hawaii)—is the *ikigai* that shapes their lives.

While researching this concept, we discovered that not a single book in the fields of psychology or personal development is dedicated to bringing this philosophy to the West.

Is *ikigai* the reason there are more centenarians in Okinawa than anywhere else? How does it inspire people to stay active until the very end? What is the secret to a long and happy life?

As we explored the matter further, we discovered that one place in particular, Ogimi, a rural town on the north end of the island with a population of three thousand, boasts the highest life expectancy in the world—a fact that has earned it the nickname the Village of Longevity.

Okinawa is where most of Japan's *shikuwasa*—a limelike fruit that packs an extraordinary antioxidant punch—comes from. Could that be Ogimi's secret to long life? Or is it the purity of the water used to brew its Moringa tea?

We decided to go study the secrets of the Japanese centenarians in person. After a year of preliminary research we arrived in the village—where residents speak an ancient dialect and practice an animist religion that features long-haired forest sprites called bunagaya—with our cameras and recording devices in hand. As soon as we arrived we could sense the incredible friendliness of its residents, who laughed and joked incessantly amid lush green hills fed by crystalline waters.

As we conducted our interviews with the eldest residents of the town, we realized that something far more powerful than just these natural resources was at work: an uncommon joy flows from its inhabitants and guides them through the long and pleasurable journey of their lives.

Again, the mysterious *ikigai*.

But what is it, exactly? How do you get it?

It never ceased to surprise us that this haven of nearly eternal life was located precisely in Okinawa, where two hundred thousand innocent lives were lost at the end of World War II. Rather than harbor animosity toward outsiders, however, Okinawans live by the principle of *ichariba chode*, a local expression that means "treat everyone like a brother, even if you've never met them before."

It turns out that one of the secrets to happiness of Ogimi's residents is feeling like part of a community. From an early age they practice *yuimaaru*, or teamwork, and so are used to helping one another.

Nurturing friendships, eating light, getting enough rest, and doing regular, moderate exercise are all part of the equation of good health, but at the heart of the joie de vivre that inspires these centenarians to keep celebrating birthdays and cherishing each new day is their *ikigai*.

The purpose of this book is to bring the secrets of Japan's

centenarians to you and give you the tools to find your own *ikigai*.

Because those who discover their *ikigai* have everything they need for a long and joyful journey through life.

Happy travels!

HÉCTOR GARCÍA AND FRANCESC MIRALLES

IKIGAI

The art of
staying young while
growing old

What is your reason for being?

According to the Japanese, everyone has an *ikigai*—what a French philosopher might call a raison d'être. Some people have found their *ikigai*, while others are still looking, though they carry it within them.

Our *ikigai* is hidden deep inside each of us, and finding it requires a patient search. According to those born on Okinawa, the island with the most centenarians in the world, our *ikigai* is the reason we get up in the morning.

Based on a diagram by Mark Winn

Whatever you do, don't retire!

Having a clearly defined *ikigai* brings satisfaction, happiness, and meaning to our lives. The purpose of this book is to help you find yours, and to share insights from Japanese philosophy on the lasting health of body, mind, and spirit.

One surprising thing you notice, living in Japan, is how active people remain after they retire. In fact, many Japanese people never really retire—they keep doing what they love for as long as their health allows.

There is, in fact, no word in Japanese that means *retire* in the sense of "leaving the workforce for good" as in English. According to Dan Buettner, a *National Geographic* reporter who knows the country well, having a purpose in life is so important in Japanese culture that our idea of retirement simply doesn't exist there.

The island of (almost) eternal youth

Certain longevity studies suggest that a strong sense of community and a clearly defined *ikigai* are just as important as the famously healthful Japanese diet—perhaps even more so. Recent medical studies of centenarians from Okinawa and other so-called Blue Zones—the geographic regions where people live longest—provide a number of interesting facts about these extraordinary human beings:

- Not only do they live much longer than the rest of the world's population, they also suffer from fewer chronic illnesses such as cancer and heart disease; inflammatory disorders are also less common.
- Many of these centenarians enjoy enviable levels of vitality and health that would be unthinkable for people of advanced age elsewhere.
- Their blood tests reveal fewer free radicals (which are responsible for cellular aging), as a result of drinking tea and eating until their stomachs are only 80 percent full.
- Women experience more moderate symptoms during menopause, and both men and women maintain higher levels of sexual hormones until much later in life.
- The rate of dementia is well below the global average.

The Characters Behind *Ikigai*

In Japanese, *ikigai* is written as 生き甲斐, combining 生き, which means "life," with 甲斐, which means "to be worthwhile." 甲斐 can be broken down into the characters 甲, which means "armor," "number one," and "to be the first" (to head into battle, taking initiative as a leader), and 斐, which means "beautiful" or "elegant."

Though we will consider each of these findings over the course of the book, research clearly indicates that the Okinawans' focus on *ikigai* gives a sense of purpose to each and every day and plays an important role in their health and longevity.

The five Blue Zones

Okinawa holds first place among the world's Blue Zones. In Okinawa, women in particular live longer and have fewer diseases than anywhere else in the world. The five regions identified and analyzed by Dan Buettner in his book *The Blue Zones* are:

1. *Okinawa, Japan* (especially the northern part of the island). The locals eat a diet rich in vegetables and tofu typically served on small plates. In addition to their philosophy of *ikigai*, the *moai*, or close-knit group of friends (see page 15), plays an important role in their longevity.
2. *Sardinia, Italy* (specifically the provinces of Nuoro and Ogliastra). Locals on this island consume plenty of vegetables and one or two glasses of wine per day. As in Okinawa, the

cohesive nature of this community is another factor directly related to longevity.

3. *Loma Linda, California.* Researchers studied a group of Seventh-day Adventists who are among the longest-living people in the United States.

4. *The Nicoya Peninsula, Costa Rica.* Locals remain remarkably active after ninety; many of the region's older residents have no problem getting up at five thirty in the morning to work in the fields.

5. *Ikaria, Greece.* One of every three inhabitants of this island near the coast of Turkey is over ninety years old (compared to less than 1 percent of the population of the United States), a fact that has earned it the nickname the Island of Long Life. The local secret seems to be a lifestyle that dates back to 500 BC.

In the following chapters, we will examine several factors that seem to be the keys to longevity and are found across the Blue Zones, paying special attention to Okinawa and its so-called Village of Longevity. First, however, it is worth pointing out that three of these regions are islands, where resources can be scarce and communities have to help one another.

For many, helping others might be an *ikigai* strong enough to keep them alive.

According to scientists who have studied the five Blue Zones, the keys to longevity are diet, exercise, finding a purpose in life (an *ikigai*), and forming strong social ties—that is, having a broad circle of friends and good family relations.

Members of these communities manage their time well in order to reduce stress, consume little meat or processed foods, and drink alcohol in moderation.[1]

They don't do strenuous exercise, but they do move every day, taking walks and working in their vegetable gardens. People in the Blue Zones would rather walk than drive. Gardening, which involves daily low-intensity movement, is a practice almost all of them have in common.

The 80 percent secret

One of the most common sayings in Japan is "Hara hachi bu," which is repeated before or after eating and means something like "Fill your belly to 80 percent." Ancient wisdom advises against eating until we are full. This is why Okinawans stop eating when they feel their stomachs reach 80 percent of their capacity, rather than overeating and wearing down their bodies with long digestive processes that accelerate cellular oxidation.

Of course, there is no way to know objectively if your stomach is at 80 percent capacity. The lesson to learn from this saying is that we should stop eating when we are starting to feel full. The extra side dish, the snack we eat when we know in our hearts we don't really need it, the apple pie after lunch—all these will give us pleasure in the short term, but not having them will make us happier in the long term.

The way food is served is also important. By presenting their meals on many small plates, the Japanese tend to eat less. A typical meal in a restaurant in Japan is served in five plates on a tray, four of them very small and the main dish slightly bigger. Having five plates in front of you makes it seem like you are going to eat a lot, but what happens most of the time is that you end up feeling slightly hungry. This is one of the reasons why Westerners in Japan typically lose weight and stay trim.

Recent studies by nutritionists reveal that Okinawans consume a daily average of 1,800 to 1,900 calories, compared to 2,200 to 3,300 in the United States, and have a body mass index between 18 and 22, compared to 26 or 27 in the United States.

The Okinawan diet is rich in tofu, sweet potatoes, fish (three times per week), and vegetables (roughly 11 ounces per day). In the chapter dedicated to nutrition we will see which healthy, antioxidant-rich foods are included in this 80 percent.

Moai: Connected for life

It is customary in Okinawa to form close bonds within local communities. A *moai* is an informal group of people with common interests who look out for one another. For many, serving the community becomes part of their *ikigai*.

The *moai* has its origins in hard times, when farmers would get together to share best practices and help one another cope with meager harvests.

Members of a *moai* make a set monthly contribution to the group. This payment allows them to participate in meetings, dinners, games of go and *shogi* (Japanese chess), or whatever hobby they have in common.

The funds collected by the group are used for activities, but if there is money left over, one member (decided on a rotating basis) receives a set amount from the surplus. In this way, being part of a *moai* helps maintain emotional and financial stability. If a member of a *moai* is in financial trouble, he or she can get an advance from the group's savings. While the details of each *moai*'s accounting practices vary according to the group and its economic means, the feeling of belonging and support gives the individual a sense of security and helps increase life expectancy.

FOLLOWING THIS BRIEF introduction to the topics covered in this book, we look at a few causes of premature aging in modern life, and then explore different factors related to *ikigai*.

II

ANTIAGING SECRETS

Little things that add up
to a long and happy life

Aging's escape velocity

For more than a century, we've managed to add an average of 0.3 years to our life expectancy every year. But what would happen if we had the technology to add a year of life expectancy every year? In theory, we would achieve biological immortality, having reached aging's "escape velocity."

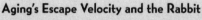

Aging's Escape Velocity and the Rabbit

Imagine a sign far off in the future with a number on it that represents the age of your death. Every year that you live, you advance closer to the sign. When you reach the sign, you die.

Now imagine a rabbit holding the sign and walking to the future. Every year that you live, the rabbit is half a year as far away. After a while, you will reach the rabbit and die.

But what if the rabbit could walk at a pace of one year for every year of your life? You would never be able to catch the rabbit, and therefore you would never die.

The speed at which the rabbit walks to the future is our technology. The more we advance technology and knowledge of our bodies, the faster we can make the rabbit walk.

Aging's escape velocity is the moment at which the rabbit walks at a pace of one year per year or faster, and we become immortal.

Researchers with an eye to the future, such as Ray Kurzweil and Aubrey de Grey, claim that we'll reach this escape velocity in a matter of decades. Other scientists are less optimistic, predicting that we'll reach a limit, a maximum age we won't be able to surpass, no matter how much technology we have. For example, some biologists assert that our cells stop regenerating after about 120 years.

Active mind, youthful body

There is much wisdom in the classic saying "mens sana in corpore sano" ("a sound mind in a sound body"): It reminds us that both mind and body are important, and that the health of one is connected to that of the other. It has been shown that maintaining an active, adaptable mind is one of the key factors in staying young.

Having a youthful mind also drives you toward a healthy lifestyle that will slow the aging process.

Just as a lack of physical exercise has negative effects on our bodies and mood, a lack of mental exercise is bad for us because it causes our neurons and neural connections to deteriorate—and, as a result, reduces our ability to react to our surroundings.

This is why it's so important to give your brain a workout. One pioneer in advocating for mental exercise is the

Israeli neuroscientist Shlomo Breznitz, who argues that the brain needs a lot of stimulation in order to stay in shape. As he stated in an interview with Eduard Punset for the Spanish television program *Redes*:

> There is a tension between what is good for someone and what they want to do. This is because people, especially older people, like to do things as they've always done them. The problem is that when the brain develops ingrained habits, it doesn't need to think anymore. Things get done quickly and efficiently on automatic pilot, often in a very advantageous way. This creates a tendency to stick to routines, and the only way of breaking these is to confront the brain with new information.[1]

Presented with new information, the brain creates new connections and is revitalized. This is why it is so important to expose yourself to change, even if stepping outside your comfort zone means feeling a bit of anxiety.

The effects of mental training have been scientifically demonstrated. According to Collins Hemingway and Shlomo Breznitz in their book *Maximum Brainpower: Challenging the Brain for Health and Wisdom*, mental training is beneficial on many levels: "You begin exercising your brain by doing a certain task for the first time," he writes. "And at first it seems very difficult, but as you learn how to do it, the training is already working. The second time, you realize that it's easier, not harder, to do, because you're getting better at it. This has a fantastic effect on a person's mood. In and of itself, it is a transformation that affects not only the results obtained, but also his or her self-image."

This description of a "mental workout" might sound a bit formal, but simply interacting with others—playing a game, for example—offers new stimuli and helps prevent the depression that can come with solitude.

Our neurons start to age while we are still in our twenties. This process is slowed, however, by intellectual activity, curiosity, and a desire to learn. Dealing with new situations, learning something new every day, playing games, and interacting with other people seem to be essential antiaging strategies for the mind. Furthermore, a more positive outlook in this regard will yield greater mental benefits.

Stress: Accused of killing longevity

Many people seem older than they are. Research into the causes of premature aging has shown that stress has a lot to do with it, because the body wears down much faster during periods of crisis. The American Institute of Stress investigated this degenerative process and concluded that *most health problems are caused by stress.*

Researchers at the Heidelberg University Hospital conducted a study in which they subjected a young doctor to a job interview, which they made even more stressful by forcing him to solve complex math problems for thirty minutes. Afterward, they took a blood sample. What they discovered was that his antibodies had reacted to stress the same way they react to pathogens, activating the proteins that trigger an immune response. The problem is that this response not only neutralizes harmful agents, it also damages healthy cells, leading them to age prematurely.

The University of California conducted a similar study, taking data and samples from thirty-nine women who had high levels of stress due to the illness of one of their children and comparing them to samples from women with healthy children and low levels of stress. They found that stress promotes cellular aging by weakening cell structures known as telomeres, which affect cellular regeneration and how our cells age. As the study revealed, the greater the stress, the greater the degenerative effect on cells.

How does stress work?

These days, people live at a frantic pace and in a nearly constant state of competition. At this fever pitch, stress is a natural response to the information being received by the body as potentially dangerous or problematic.

Theoretically, this is a useful reaction, as it helps us survive in hostile surroundings. Over the course of our evolution, we have used this response to deal with difficult situations and to flee from predators.

The alarm that goes off in our head makes our neurons activate the pituitary gland, which produces hormones that release corticotropin, which in turn circulates through the body via the sympathetic nervous system. The adrenal gland is then triggered to release adrenaline and cortisol. Adrenaline raises our respiratory rate and pulse and prepares our muscles for action, getting the body ready to react to perceived danger, while cortisol increases the release of dopamine and blood glucose, which is what gets us "charged up" and allows us to face challenges.

Cave Dwellers	Modern Humans
Were relaxed most of the time.	Work most of the time and are alert to any and all threats.
Felt stress only in very specific situations.	Are online or waiting for notifications from their cell phones twenty-four hours a day.
The threats were real: A predator could end their lives at any moment.	The brain associates the ping of a cell phone or an e-mail notification with the threat of a predator.

Cave Dwellers	Modern Humans
High doses of cortisol and adrenaline at moments of danger kept the body healthy.	Low doses of cortisol flow constantly through the body, with implications for a range of health problems, including adrenal fatigue and chronic fatigue syndrome.

These processes are, in moderation, beneficial—they help us overcome challenges in our daily lives. Nonetheless, the stress to which human beings are subjected today is clearly harmful.

Stress has a degenerative effect over time. A sustained state of emergency affects the neurons associated with memory, as well as inhibiting the release of certain hormones, the absence of which can cause depression. Its secondary effects include irritability, insomnia, anxiety, and high blood pressure.

As such, though challenges are good for keeping mind and body active, we should adjust our high-stress lifestyles in order to avoid the premature aging of our bodies.

Be mindful about reducing stress

Whether or not the threats we perceive are real, stress is an easily identifiable condition that not only causes anxiety but is also highly psychosomatic, affecting everything from our digestive system to our skin.

This is why prevention is so important in avoiding the toll that stress takes on us—and why many experts recommend practicing mindfulness.

The central premise of this stress-reduction method is focusing on the self: noticing our responses, even if they are conditioned by habit, in order to be fully conscious of them. In this way, we connect with the here and now and limit thoughts that tend to spiral out of control.

"We have to learn to turn off the autopilot that's steering us in an endless loop. We all know people who snack while talking on the phone or watching the news. You ask them if the omelet they just ate had onion in it, and they can't tell you," says Roberto Alcibar, who abandoned his fast-paced life to become a certified instructor of mindfulness after an illness threw him into a period of acute stress.

One way to reach a state of mindfulness is through meditation, which helps filter the information that reaches us from the outside world. It can also be achieved through breathing exercises, yoga, and body scans.

Achieving mindfulness involves a gradual process of training, but with a bit of practice we can learn to focus our mind completely, which reduces stress and helps us live longer.

A little stress is good for you

While sustained, intense stress is a known enemy of longevity and both mental and physical health, low levels of stress have been shown to be beneficial.

After observing a group of test subjects for more than twenty years, Dr. Howard S. Friedman, a psychology professor at the University of California, Riverside, discovered that people who maintained a low level of stress, who faced challenges and put their heart and soul into their work in order to succeed, lived longer than those who chose a more relaxed lifestyle and retired earlier. From this, he concluded that a small dose of stress is a positive thing, as those who live with low levels of stress tend to develop healthier habits, smoke less, and drink less alcohol.[2]

Given this, it is not surprising that many of the supercentenarians—people who live to be 110 or more—whom we'll meet in this book talk about having lived intense lives and working well into old age.

A lot of sitting will age you

In the Western world in particular, the rise in sedentary behavior has led to numerous diseases such as hypertension and obesity, which in turn affect longevity.

Spending too much time seated at work or at home not only reduces muscular and respiratory fitness but also increases appetite and curbs the desire to participate in activities. Being sedentary can lead to hypertension, imbalanced eating, cardiovascular disease, osteoporosis, and even certain kinds of cancer. Recent studies have shown a connection between a lack of physical activity and the progressive distortion of telomeres in the immune system, which ages those cells and, in turn, the organism as a whole.

This is a problem at all life stages, not only among adults. Sedentary children suffer from high rates of obesity and all its associated health issues and risks, which is why it's so important to develop a healthy and active lifestyle at an early age.

It's easy to be less sedentary; it just takes a bit of effort and a few changes to your routine. We can access a more active lifestyle that makes us feel better inside and out—we just have to add a few ingredients to our everyday habits:

- *Walk to work, or just go on a walk* for at least twenty minutes each day.
- *Use your feet instead of an elevator or escalator.* This is good for your posture, your muscles, and your respiratory system, among other things.
- *Participate in social or leisure activities* so that you don't spend too much time in front of the television.

- *Replace your junk food with fruit* and you'll have less of an urge to snack, and more nutrients in your system.
- *Get the right amount of sleep.* Seven to nine hours is good, but any more than that makes us lethargic.
- *Play with children or pets, or join a sports team.* This not only strengthens the body but also stimulates the mind and boosts self-esteem.
- *Be conscious of your daily routine* in order to detect harmful habits and replace them with more positive ones.

By making these small changes, we can begin to renew our bodies and minds and increase our life expectancy.

A model's best-kept secret

Though we age both externally and internally, both physically and mentally, one of the things that tell us the most about people's age is their skin, which takes on different textures and colors according to processes going on beneath the surface. Most of those who make their living as models claim to sleep between nine and ten hours the night before a fashion show. This gives their skin a taut, wrinkle-free appearance and a healthy, radiant glow.

Science has shown that sleep is a key antiaging tool, because when we sleep we generate melatonin, a hormone that occurs naturally in our bodies. The pineal gland produces it from the neurotransmitter serotonin according to our diurnal and nocturnal rhythms, and it plays a role in our sleep and waking cycles.

A powerful antioxidant, melatonin helps us live longer, and also offers the following benefits:

- It strengthens the immune system.
- It contains an element that protects against cancer.
- It promotes the natural production of insulin.
- It slows the onset of Alzheimer's disease.
- It helps prevent osteoporosis and fight heart disease.

For all these reasons, melatonin is a great ally in preserving youth. It should be noted, however, that melatonin production decreases after age thirty. We can compensate for this by:

- Eating a balanced diet and getting more calcium.
- Soaking up a moderate amount of sun each day.
- Getting enough sleep.
- Avoiding stress, alcohol, tobacco, and caffeine, all of which make it harder to get a good night's rest, depriving us of the melatonin we need.

Experts are trying to determine whether artificially stimulating production of melatonin might help slow the aging process . . . which would confirm the theory that we already carry the secret to longevity within us.

Antiaging attitudes

The mind has tremendous power over the body and how quickly it ages. Most doctors agree that the secret to keeping the body young is keeping the mind active—a key element of *ikigai*—and in not caving in when we face difficulties throughout our lives.

One study, conducted at Yeshiva University, found that the people who live the longest have two dispositional traits in common: a *positive attitude* and a high degree of *emotional awareness*. In other words, those who face challenges with a positive outlook and are able to manage their emotions are already well on their way toward longevity.

A *stoic attitude*—serenity in the face of a setback—can also help keep you young, as it lowers anxiety and stress levels and stabilizes behavior. This can be seen in the greater life expectancies of certain cultures with unhurried, deliberate lifestyles.

Many centenarians and supercentenarians have similar

profiles: They have had full lives that were difficult at times, but they knew how to approach these challenges with a positive attitude and not be overwhelmed by the obstacles they faced.

Alexander Imich, who in 2014 became the world's oldest living man at age 111, knew he had good genes but understood that other factors contributed, too: "The life you live is equally or more important for longevity," he said in an interview with Reuters after being added to *Guinness World Records* in 2014.

An ode to longevity

During our stay in Ogimi, the village that holds the Guinness record for longevity, a woman who was about to turn 100 years old sang the following song for us in a mixture of Japanese and the local dialect:

To keep healthy and have a long life,
eat just a little of everything with relish,
go to bed early, get up early, and then go out for a walk.
We live each day with serenity and we enjoy the journey.
To keep healthy and have a long life,
we get on well with all of our friends.
Spring, summer, fall, winter,

we happily enjoy all the seasons.

The secret is to not get distracted by how old the fingers are;
from the fingers to the head and back once again.

If you keep moving with your fingers working, 100 years
   will come to you.*

We can now use our fingers to turn the page to the next
chapter, where we will look at the close relationship between
longevity and discovering our life's mission.

---

* English translation by Steven Tolliver.

FROM LOGOTHERAPY TO IKIGAI

How to live longer and better by finding your purpose

What is logotherapy?

A colleague once asked Viktor Frankl to define his school of psychology in a single phrase, to which Frankl replied, "Well, in logotherapy the patient sits up straight and has to listen to things that are, on occasion, hard to hear." The colleague had just described psychoanalysis to him in the following terms: "In psychoanalysis, the patient lies down on a couch and tells you things that are, on occasion, hard to say."

Frankl explains that one of the first questions he would ask his patients was "Why do you not commit suicide?" Usually the patient found good reasons not to, and was able to carry on. What, then, does logotherapy do? [1]

The answer is pretty clear: *It helps you find reasons to live.*

Logotherapy pushes patients to consciously discover their life's purpose in order to confront their neuroses. Their quest to fulfill their destiny then motivates them to press forward, breaking the mental chains of the past and overcoming whatever obstacles they encounter along the way.

Something to Live For

A study conducted by Frankl in his Vienna clinic found that among both patients and personnel, around 80 percent believed that human beings needed a reason for living, and around 60 percent felt they had someone or something in their lives worth dying for.[2]

The search for meaning

The search for purpose became a personal, driving force that allowed Frankl to achieve his goals. The process of logotherapy can be summarized in these five steps:

1. A person feels empty, frustrated, or anxious.
2. The therapist shows him that what he is feeling is the desire to have a meaningful life.
3. The patient discovers his life's purpose (at that particular point in time).
4. Of his own free will, the patient decides to accept or reject that destiny.
5. This newfound passion for life helps him overcome obstacles and sorrows.

Frankl himself would live and die for his principles and ideals. His experiences as a prisoner at Auschwitz showed him that "Everything can be taken from a man but one thing: the last of the human freedoms—to choose one's attitude in any given set of circumstances, to choose one's own way."[3] It was something he had to go through alone, without any help, and it inspired him for the rest of his life.

Ten Differences Between Psychoanalysis and Logotherapy	
Psychoanalysis	Logotherapy
The patient reclines on a couch, like a patient.	The patient sits facing the therapist, who guides him or her without passing judgment.
Is retrospective: It looks to the past.	Looks toward the future.
Is introspective: It analyzes neuroses.	Does not delve into the patient's neuroses.
The drive is toward pleasure.	The drive is toward purpose and meaning.
Centers on psychology.	Includes a spiritual dimension.
Works on psychogenic neuroses.	Also works on noogenic, or existential, neuroses.
Analyzes the unconscious origin of conflicts (instinctual dimension).	Deals with conflicts when and where they arise (spiritual dimension).
Limits itself to the patient's instincts.	Also deals with spiritual realities.
Is fundamentally incompatible with faith.	Is compatible with faith.
Seeks to reconcile conflicts and satisfy impulses and instincts.	Seeks to help the patient find meaning in his life and satisfy his moral principles.

Fight for yourself

Existential frustration arises when our life is without purpose, or when that purpose is skewed. In Frankl's view, however, there is no need to see this frustration as an anomaly or a symptom of neurosis; instead, it can be a positive thing—a catalyst for change.

Logotherapy does not see this frustration as *mental illness*, the way other forms of therapy do, but rather as *spiritual anguish*—a natural and beneficial phenomenon that drives those who suffer from it to seek a cure, whether on their own or with the help of others, and in so doing to find greater satisfaction in life. It helps them change their own destiny.

Logotherapy enters the picture if the person needs help doing this, if he needs guidance in discovering his life's purpose and later in overcoming conflicts so he can keep moving toward his objective. In *Man's Search for Meaning*, Frankl cites one of Nietzsche's famous aphorisms: "He who has a *why* to live for can bear with almost any *how*."

Based on his own experience, Frankl believed that our health depends on that natural tension that comes from comparing what we've accomplished so far with what we'd like to achieve in the future. What we need, then, is not a peaceful existence, but a challenge we can strive to meet by applying all the skills at our disposal.

Existential crisis, on the other hand, is typical of modern societies in which people do what they are told to do, or what others do, rather than what they want to do. They often try to fill the gap between what is expected of them and what they want for themselves with economic power or physical pleasure, or by numbing their senses. It can even lead to suicide.

Sunday neurosis, for example, is what happens when, without the obligations and commitments of the workweek, the individual realizes how empty he is inside. He has to find a solution. Above all, he has to find his purpose, his reason for getting out of bed—his *ikigai*.

"I Feel Empty Inside"
In a study conducted at the Vienna Polyclinic Hospital, Frankl's team found that 55 percent of the patients they interviewed were experiencing some degree of existential crisis.[4]

According to logotherapy, discovering one's purpose in life helps an individual fill that existential void. Frankl, a man who faced his problems and turned his objectives into actions, could look back on his life in peace as he grew old. He did not have to envy those still enjoying their youth, because he had amassed a broad set of experiences that showed he had lived *for something*.

Better living through logotherapy: A few key ideas

- We don't *create* the meaning of our life, as Sartre claimed— we *discover* it.
- We each have a unique reason for being, which can be adjusted or transformed many times over the years.
- Just as worry often brings about precisely the thing that was feared, excessive attention to a desire (or "hyper- intention") can keep that desire from being fulfilled.
- Humor can help break negative cycles and reduce anxiety.
- We all have the capacity to do noble or terrible things. The side of the equation we end up on depends on our decisions, not on the condition in which we find ourselves.

In the pages that follow, we will look at four cases from Frankl's own practice in order to better understand the search for meaning and purpose.

Case study: Viktor Frankl

In German concentration camps, as in those that would later be built in Japan and Korea, psychiatrists confirmed that the prisoners with the greatest chance of survival were those who had things they wanted to accomplish outside the camp, those who felt a strong need to get out of there alive. This was true of Frankl, who, after being released and successfully developing the school of logotherapy, realized he had been the first patient of his own practice.

Frankl had a goal to achieve, and it made him persevere. He arrived at Auschwitz carrying a manuscript that contained all the theories and research he had compiled over the course of his career, ready for publication. When it was confiscated, he felt compelled to write it all over again, and that need drove him and gave his life meaning amid the constant horror and doubt of the concentration camp—so much so that over the years, and especially when he fell ill with typhus, he would jot down fragments and key words from the lost work on any scrap of paper he found.

Case study: The American diplomat

An important North American diplomat went to Frankl to pick up where he left off with a course of treatment he had started five years earlier in the United States. When Frankl asked him why he'd started therapy in the first place, the diplomat answered that he hated his job and his country's international policies, which he had to follow and enforce. His American psychoanalyst, whom he'd been seeing for years, insisted he make peace with his father so that his government and his job, both representations of the paternal figure, would seem less disagreeable. Frankl, however, showed him in just a few sessions that his frustration was due to the fact that he wanted to pursue a different career, and the diplomat concluded his treatment with that idea in mind.

Five years later, the former diplomat informed Frankl that he had been working during that time in a different profession, and that he was happy.

In Frankl's view, the man not only didn't need all those years of psychoanalysis, he also couldn't even really be considered a "patient" in need of therapy. He was simply someone in search of a new life's purpose; as soon as he found it, his life took on deeper meaning.

Case study: The suicidal mother

The mother of a boy who had died at age eleven was admitted to Frankl's clinic after she tried to kill herself and her other son. It was this other son, paralyzed since birth, who kept her from carrying out her plan: He *did* believe his life had a purpose, and if his mother killed them both, it would keep him from achieving his goals.

The woman shared her story in a group session. To help her, Frankl asked another woman to imagine a hypothetical situation in which she lay on her deathbed, old and wealthy but childless. The woman insisted that, in that case, she would have felt her life had been a failure.

When the suicidal mother was asked to perform the same exercise, imagining herself on her deathbed, she looked back and realized that she had done everything in her power for her children—for both of them. She had given her paralyzed son a good life, and he had turned into a kind, reasonably happy person. To this she added, crying, "As for myself, I can look back peacefully on my life; for I can say my life was full of meaning, and I have tried hard to live it fully; I have done my best—I have done my best for my son. My life was no failure!"

In this way, by imagining herself on her deathbed and looking back, the suicidal mother found the meaning that, though she was not aware of it, her life already had.

Case study: The grief-stricken doctor

An elderly doctor, unable to overcome the deep depression into which he'd fallen after the death of his wife two years earlier, went to Frankl for help.

Instead of giving him advice or analyzing his condition, Frankl asked him what would have happened if he had been the one who died first. The doctor, horrified, answered that it would have been terrible for his poor wife, that she would have suffered tremendously. To which Frankl responded, "You see, doctor? You have spared her all that suffering, but the price you have to pay for this is to survive, and mourn her."

The doctor didn't say another word. He left Frankl's office in peace, after taking the therapist's hand in his own. He was able to tolerate the pain in place of his beloved wife. His life had been given a purpose.

Morita therapy

In the same decade that logotherapy came into being—a few years earlier, in fact—Shoma Morita created his own purpose-centered therapy, in Japan. It proved to be effective in the treatment of neurosis, obsessive-compulsive disorder, and posttraumatic stress.

In addition to being a psychotherapist, Shoma Morita was a Zen Buddhist, and his therapy left a lasting spiritual mark on Japan.

Many Western forms of therapy focus on controlling or modifying the patient's emotions. In the West, we tend to believe that what we think influences how we feel, which in turn influences how we act. In contrast, Morita therapy focuses on teaching patients to *accept their emotions without trying to control them*, since their feelings will change *as a result of their actions*.

In addition to accepting the patient's emotions, Morita therapy seeks to "create" new emotions on the basis of actions. According to Morita, these emotions are learned through experience and repetition.

Morita therapy is not meant to eliminate symptoms; instead it teaches us to accept our desires, anxieties, fears, and worries, and let them go. As Morita writes in his book *Morita Therapy and the True Nature of Anxiety-Based Disorders*, "In feelings, it is best to be wealthy and generous."

Morita explained the idea of letting go of negative feelings with the following fable: A donkey that is tied to a post by a rope will keep walking around the post in an attempt to free itself, only to become more immobilized and attached to the post. The same thing applies to people with obsessive thinking who become more trapped in their own suffering when they try to escape from their fears and discomfort.[5]

The basic principles of Morita therapy

1. Accept your feelings. If we have obsessive thoughts, we should not try to control them or get rid of them. If we do, they become more intense. Regarding human emotions, the Zen master would say, "If we try to get rid of one wave with another, we end up with an infinite sea." We don't create our feelings; they simply come to us, and we have to accept them. The trick is welcoming them. Morita likened emotions to the weather:

We can't predict or control them; we can only observe them. To this point, he often quoted the Vietnamese monk Thich Nhat Hanh, who would say, "Hello, solitude. How are you today? Come, sit with me, and I will care for you."[6]

2. *Do what you should be doing.* We shouldn't focus on eliminating symptoms, because recovery will come on its own. We should focus instead on the present moment, and if we are suffering, on accepting that suffering. Above all, we should avoid intellectualizing the situation. The therapist's mission is to develop the patient's character so he or she can face any situation, and character is grounded in the things we do. Morita therapy does not offer its patients explanations, but rather allows them to learn from their actions and activities. It doesn't tell you how to meditate, or how to keep a diary the way Western therapies do. It is up to the patient to make discoveries through experience.

3. *Discover your life's purpose.* We can't control our emotions, but we can take charge of our actions every day. This is why we should have a clear sense of our purpose, and always keep Morita's mantra in mind: "What do we need to be doing right now? What action should we be taking?" The key to achieving this is having dared to look inside yourself to find your *ikigai*.

The four phases of Morita therapy

Morita's original treatment, which lasts fifteen to twenty-one days, consists of the following stages:

1. Isolation and rest (five to seven days). During the first week of treatment, the patient rests in a room without any external stimuli. No television, books, family, friends, or speaking. All the patient has is his thoughts. He lies down for most of the day and is visited regularly by the therapist, who tries to avoid interacting with him as much as possible. The therapist simply advises the patient to continue observing the rise and fall of his emotions as he lies there. When the patient gets bored and wants to start doing things again, he is ready to move on to the next stage of therapy.

2. Light occupational therapy (five to seven days). In this stage, the patient performs repetitive tasks in silence. One of these is keeping a diary about his thoughts and feelings. The patient goes outside after a week of being shut in, takes walks in nature, and does breathing exercises. He also starts doing simple activities, such as gardening, drawing, or painting. During this stage, the patient is still not allowed to talk to anyone, except the therapist.

3. Occupational therapy (five to seven days). In this stage, the patient performs tasks that require physical movement. Dr. Morita liked to take his patients to the mountains to chop wood. In addition to physical tasks, the patient is also immersed in other activities, such as writing, painting, or making ceramics. The patient can speak with others at this stage, but only about the tasks at hand.

4. The return to social life and the "real" world. The patient leaves the hospital and is reintroduced to social life, but maintains the practices of meditation and occupational therapy developed during treatment. The idea is to reenter society as a new person, with a sense of purpose, and without being controlled by social or emotional pressures.

Naikan meditation

Morita was a great Zen master of Naikan introspective meditation. Much of his therapy draws on his knowledge and mastery of this school, which centers on three questions the individual must ask him- or herself:

1. What have I received from person X?
2. What have I given to person X?
3. What problems have I caused person X?

Through these reflections, we stop identifying others as the cause of our problems and deepen our own sense of responsibility. As Morita said, "If you are angry and want to fight, think about it for three days before coming to blows. After three days, the intense desire to fight will pass on its own."[7]

And now, *ikigai*

Logotherapy and Morita therapy are both grounded in a personal, unique experience that you can access without therapists or spiritual retreats: the mission of finding your *ikigai*, your existential fuel. Once you find it, it is only a matter of having the courage and making the effort to stay on the right path.

In the following chapters, we'll take a look at the basic tools you'll need to get moving along that path: finding flow in the tasks you've chosen to do, eating in a balanced and mindful way, doing low-intensity exercise, and learning not to give in when difficulties arise. In order to do this, you have to accept that the world—like the people who live in it—is imperfect, but that it is still full of opportunities for growth and achievement.

Are you ready to throw yourself into your passion as if it were the most important thing in the world?

**FIND FLOW IN EVERYTHING
YOU DO**

How to turn work and
free time into spaces
for growth

We are what we repeatedly do.
Excellence, then, is not an act but a habit.

—Aristotle

Going with the flow

Imagine you are skiing down one of your favorite slopes. Powdery snow flies up on both sides of you like white sand. Conditions are perfect.

You are entirely focused on skiing as well as you can. You know exactly how to move at each moment. *There is no future, no past. There is only the present.* You feel the snow, your skis, your body, and your consciousness united as a single entity. *You are completely immersed in the experience, not thinking about or distracted by anything else.* Your ego dissolves, and you become part of what you are doing.

This is the kind of experience Bruce Lee described with his famous "Be water, my friend."

We've all felt our sense of time vanish when we lose ourselves in an activity we enjoy. We start cooking and before we know it, several hours have passed. We spend an afternoon with a book and forget about the world going by until we notice the sunset and realize we haven't eaten dinner. We go surfing and don't realize how many hours we have spent in the water until the next day, when our muscles ache.

The opposite can also happen. When we have to complete a task we don't want to do, every minute feels like a lifetime and we can't stop looking at our watch. As the quip attributed to Einstein goes, "Put your hand on a hot stove for a minute and it seems like an hour. Sit with a pretty girl for an hour, and it seems like a minute. That is relativity."

The funny thing is that someone else might really enjoy the same task, but we want to finish as quickly as possible.

What makes us enjoy doing something so much that we forget about whatever worries we might have while we do it? When are we happiest? These questions can help us discover our *ikigai*.

The power of flow

These questions are also at the heart of psychologist Mihaly Csikszentmihalyi's research into the experience of being completely immersed in what we are doing. Csikszentmihalyi called this state "flow," and described it as the pleasure, delight, creativity, and process when we are completely immersed in life.

There is no magic recipe for finding happiness, for living according to your *ikigai*, but one key ingredient is the ability to reach this state of flow and, through this state, to have an "optimal experience."

In order to achieve this optimal experience, we have to focus on increasing the time we spend on activities that bring us to this state of flow, rather than allowing ourselves to get caught up in activities that offer immediate pleasure—like eating too much, abusing drugs or alcohol, or stuffing ourselves with chocolate in front of the TV.

As Csikszentmihalyi asserts in his book *Flow: The Psychology of Optimal Experience*, flow is "the state in which people are so involved in an activity that nothing else seems to matter; the experience itself is so enjoyable that people will do it even at great cost, for the sheer sake of doing it."

It is not only creative professionals who require the high doses of concentration that promote flow. Most athletes, chess players, and engineers also spend much of their time on activities that bring them to this state.

According to Csikszentmihalyi's research, a chess player feels the same way upon entering a state of flow as a mathematician working on a formula or a surgeon performing an operation. A professor of psychology, Csikszentmihalyi analyzed data from people around the world and discovered that flow is the same among individuals of all ages and cultures. In New York and Okinawa, we all reach a state of flow in the same way.

But what happens to our mind when we are in that state?

When we flow, we are focused on a concrete task without

any distractions. Our mind is "in order." The opposite occurs when we try to do something while our mind is on other things.

If you often find yourself losing focus while working on something you consider important, there are several strategies you can employ to increase your chances of achieving flow.

The Seven Conditions for Achieving Flow

According to researcher Owen Schaffer of DePaul University, the requirements for achieving flow are:

1. Knowing what to do
2. Knowing how to do it
3. Knowing how well you are doing
4. Knowing where to go (where navigation is involved)
5. Perceiving significant challenges
6. Perceiving significant skills
7. Being free from distractions[1]

Strategy 1: Choose a difficult task (but not too difficult!)

Schaffer's model encourages us to take on tasks that we have a chance of completing but that are slightly outside our comfort zone.

Every task, sport, or job has a set of rules, and we need a set of skills to follow them. If the rules for completing a task or achieving a purpose are too basic relative to our skill set, we will likely get bored. Activities that are too easy lead to apathy.

If, on the other hand, we assign ourselves a task that is too difficult, we won't have the skills to complete it and will almost certainly give up—and feel frustrated, to boot.

The ideal is to find a middle path, something aligned with our abilities but just a bit of a stretch, so we experience it as a challenge. This is what Ernest Hemingway meant when he said, "Sometimes I write better than I can."[2]

We want to see challenges through to the end because we enjoy the feeling of pushing ourselves. Bertrand Russell expressed a similar idea when he said, "To be able to concentrate for a considerable amount of time is essential to difficult achievement."[3]

If you're a graphic designer, learn a new software program for your next project. If you're a programmer, use a new programming language. If you're a dancer, try to incorporate into your next routine a movement that has seemed impossible for years.

Add a little something extra, something that takes you out of your comfort zone.

Even doing something as simple as reading means following certain rules, having certain abilities and knowledge. If we set out to read a book on quantum mechanics for specialists in physics without being specialists in physics ourselves, we'll probably give up after a few minutes. On the other end of the spectrum, if we already know everything a book has to tell us, we'll get bored right away.

However, if the book is appropriate to our knowledge and abilities, and builds on what we already know, we'll immerse ourselves in our reading, and time will flow. This pleasure and satisfaction are evidence that we are in tune with our *ikigai*.

Easy	Challenging	Beyond Our Abilities
Boredom	**Flow**	Anxiety

Strategy 2: Have a clear, concrete objective

Video games—played in moderation—board games, and sports are great ways to achieve flow, because the objective tends to be very clear: Beat your rival or your own record while following a set of explicitly defined rules.

Unfortunately, the objective isn't quite as clear in most situations.

According to a study by Boston Consulting Group, when

asked about their bosses, the number one complaint of employees at multinational corporations is that they don't "communicate the team's mission clearly," and that, as a result, the employees don't know what their objectives are.

What often happens, especially in big companies, is that the executives get lost in the details of obsessive planning, creating strategies to hide the fact that they don't have a clear objective. It's like heading out to sea with a map but no destination.

It is much more important to have a compass pointing to a concrete objective than to have a map. Joi Ito, director of the MIT Media Lab, encourages us to use the principle of "compass over maps" as a tool to navigate our world of uncertainty. In the book *Whiplash: How to Survive Our Faster Future*, he and Jeff Howe write, "In an increasingly unpredictable world moving ever more quickly, a detailed map may lead you deep into the woods at an unnecessarily high cost. A good compass, though, will always take you where you need to go. It doesn't mean that you should start your journey without any idea where you're going. What it does mean is understanding that while the path to your goal may not be straight, you'll finish faster and more efficiently than you would have if you had trudged along a preplanned route."

In business, the creative professions, and education alike, it's important to reflect on what we hope to achieve before starting to work, study, or make something. We should ask ourselves questions such as:

- What is my objective for today's session in the studio?
- How many words am I going to write today for the article coming out next month?
- What is my team's mission?
- How fast will I set the metronome tomorrow in order to play that sonata at an allegro tempo by the end of the week?

Having a clear objective is important in achieving flow, but we also have to know how to leave it behind when we get down to business. Once the journey has begun, we should keep this objective in mind without obsessing over it.

When Olympic athletes compete for a gold medal, they can't stop to think how pretty the medal is. They have to be present in the moment—they have to *flow*. If they lose focus for a second, thinking how proud they'll be to show the medal to their parents, they'll almost certainly commit an error at a critical moment and will not win the competition.

One common example of this is writer's block. Imagine that a writer has to finish a novel in three months. The objective is clear; the problem is that the writer can't stop obsessing over it. Every day she wakes up thinking, "I have to write that novel," and every day she sets about reading the newspaper and cleaning the house. Every evening she feels frustrated and promises she'll get to work the next day.

Days, weeks, and months pass, and the writer still hasn't gotten anything down on the page, when all it would have taken was to sit down and get that first word out, then the second . . . to flow with the project, expressing her *ikigai*.

As soon as you take these first small steps, your anxiety will disappear and you will achieve a pleasant flow in the activity you're doing. Getting back to Albert Einstein, "a happy man is too satisfied with the present to dwell on the future."[4]

Vague Objective	Clearly Defined Objective and a Focus on Process	Obsessive Desire to Achieve a Goal While Ignoring Process
Confusion; time and energy wasted on meaningless tasks	**Flow**	Fixation on the objective rather than getting down to business
Mental block	**Flow**	Mental block

Strategy 3: Concentrate on a single task

This is perhaps one of the greatest obstacles we face today, with so much technology and so many distractions. We're listening to a video on YouTube while writing an e-mail, when suddenly a chat prompt pops up and we answer it. Then our smartphone vibrates in our pocket; just as soon as we respond to that message, we're back at our computer, logging on to Facebook.

Pretty soon thirty minutes have passed, and we've forgotten what the e-mail we were writing was supposed to be about.

This also happens sometimes when we put on a movie with dinner and don't realize how delicious the salmon was until we're taking the last bite.

We often think that combining tasks will save us time, but scientific evidence shows that it has the opposite effect. Even those who claim to be good at multitasking are not very productive. In fact, they are some of the least productive people.

Our brains can take in millions of bits of information but can only actually process a few dozen per second. When we say we're multitasking, what we're really doing is *switching back and forth* between tasks very quickly. Unfortunately, we're not computers adept at parallel processing. We end up spending all our energy alternating between tasks, instead of focusing on doing one of them well.

Concentrating on one thing at a time may be the single most important factor in achieving flow.

According to Csikszentmihalyi, in order to focus on a task we need:

1. To be in a distraction-free environment
2. To have control over what we are doing at every moment

Technology is great, if we're in control of it. It's not so great if it takes control of us. For example, if you have to write a research paper, you might sit down at your computer and use Google to look up the information you need. However, if you're not very disciplined, you might end up surfing the Web instead of writing that paper. In that case, Google and the Internet will have taken over, pulling you out of your state of flow.

It has been scientifically shown that if we continually ask our brains to switch back and forth between tasks, we waste time, make more mistakes, and remember less of what we've done.

Several studies conducted at Stanford University by Clifford Ivar Nass describe our generation as suffering from an *epidemic of multitasking*. One such study analyzed the behavior of hundreds of students, dividing them into groups based on the number of things they tended to do at once. The students who were the most addicted to multitasking typically alternated among more than four tasks; for example, taking notes while reading a textbook, listening to a podcast, answering messages on their smartphone, and sometimes checking their Twitter timeline.

Each group of students was shown a screen with several red and several blue arrows. The objective of the exercise was to count the red arrows.

At first, all the students answered correctly right away, without much trouble. As the number of blue arrows increased (the number of red arrows stayed the same; only their position changed), however, the students accustomed to multitasking had serious trouble counting the red arrows in the time allotted, or as quickly as the students who did not habitually multitask, for one very simple reason: They got distracted by the blue arrows! Their brains were trained to pay attention to every stimulus, regardless of its importance, while the brains of the other students were trained to focus on a single task—in this case, counting the red arrows and ignoring the blue ones.[5]

Other studies indicate that working on several things at once lowers our productivity by at least 60 percent and our IQ by more than ten points.

One study funded by the Swedish Council for Working Life and Social Research found that a sample group of more than four thousand young adults between the ages of twenty and twenty-four who were addicted to their smartphones got less sleep, felt less connected to their community at school, and were more likely to show signs of depression.[6]

- Work in a space where you will not be distracted. If you can't do this at home, go to a library, a café, or, if your task involves playing the saxophone, a music studio. If you find that your surroundings continue to distract you, keep looking until you find the right place.

- Divide each activity into groups of related tasks, and assign each group its own place and time. For example, if you're writing a magazine article, you could do research and take notes at home in the morning, write in the library in the afternoon, and edit on the couch at night.

- Bundle routine tasks—such as sending out invoices, making phone calls, and so on—and do them all at once.

Advantages of Flow	Disadvantages of Distraction
A focused mind	A wandering mind
Living in the present	Thinking about the past and the future
We are free from worry	Concerns about our daily life and the people around us invade our thoughts
The hours fly by	Every minute seems endless
We feel in control	We lose control and fail to complete the task at hand, or other tasks or people keep us from our work
We prepare thoroughly	We act without being prepared

Advantages of Flow	Disadvantages of Distraction
We know what we should be doing at any given moment	We frequently get stuck and don't know how to proceed
Our mind is clear and overcomes all obstacles to the flow of thought	We are plagued by doubts, concerns, and low self-esteem
It's pleasant	It's boring and exhausting
Our ego fades: We are not the ones controlling the activity or task we're doing—the task is leading us	Constant self-criticism: Our ego is present and we feel frustrated

Flow in Japan: *Takumis*, engineers, geniuses, and *otakus*

What do *takumis* (artisans), engineers, inventors, and *otakus* (fans of anime and manga) have in common? They all understand the importance of flowing with their *ikigai* at all times.

One widespread stereotype about people in Japan is that they're exceptionally dedicated and hardworking, even though some Japanese people say they look like they're working harder than they really are. There is no doubt, though, about their ability to be completely absorbed in a task, or about their perseverance when there is a problem to be solved. One of the first words one learns when starting Japanese lessons is *ganbaru*, which means "to persevere" or "to stay firm by doing one's best."

Japanese people often apply themselves to even the most basic tasks with an intensity that borders on obsession. We see this in all kinds of contexts, from the "retirees" taking meticulous care of their rice fields in the mountains of Nagano to the college students working the weekend shift in convenience stores known as *konbinis*. If you go to Japan, you'll experience this attention to detail firsthand in almost every transaction.

Walk into one of the stores that sell handcrafted objects in Naha, Kanazawa, or Kyoto and you'll also discover that Japan is a treasure trove of traditional craftwork. The people of Japan have a unique talent for creating new technologies while preserving artisanal traditions and techniques.

The art of the *takumi*

Toyota employs "artisans" who are able to make a certain type of screw by hand. These *takumi*, or experts in a particular manual skill, are extremely important to Toyota, and they are hard to replace. Some of them are the only people who know how to perform their exact skill, and it doesn't seem as though a new generation is going to take up the mantle.

Turntable needles are another example: They're produced almost exclusively in Japan, where you can find the last remaining people who know how to use the machinery required to make these precision needles, and who are trying to pass on their knowledge to their descendants.

We met a *takumi* on a visit to Kumano, a small town near Hiroshima. We were there for the day, working on a photo essay for one of the most famous brands of makeup brushes in the West. The billboard welcoming visitors to Kumano shows a mascot holding a large brush. In addition to the brush factories, the town is full of little houses and vegetable gardens; heading farther in, you can see several Shinto shrines at the base of the mountains that surround the town.

We spent hours taking photos in factories full of people in orderly rows, each doing a single task—such as painting the handles of the brushes or loading boxes of them onto trucks—before we realized we still hadn't seen anyone actually putting bristles into the brush heads.

After we asked about this and got the runaround several times, the president of one company agreed to show us how it was done. He led us out of the building and asked us to get into his car. After a five-minute drive we parked next to another, smaller structure and climbed the stairs. He opened a door and we walked into a small room filled with windows that let in lovely natural light.

In the middle of the room was a woman wearing a mask. You could see only her eyes. She was so focused on choosing individual bristles for the brushes—gracefully moving her hands and fingers, using scissors and combs to sort the bristles—that she didn't even notice our presence. Her movements were so quick it was hard to tell what she was doing.

The president of the company interrupted her to let her know that we'd be taking photos as she worked. We couldn't see her mouth, but the glint in her eye and the cheerful in-flection in her speech let us know she was smiling. She looked happy and proud talking about her work and responsibilities.

We had to use extremely fast shutter speeds to capture her movements. Her hands danced and *flowed* in concert with her tools and the bristles she was sorting.

The president told us that this *takumi* was one of the most important people in the company, even though she was hidden away in a separate building. Every bristle of every brush the company made passed through her hands.

Steve Jobs in Japan

Apple cofounder Steve Jobs was a big fan of Japan. Not only did he visit the Sony factories in the 1980s and adopt many of their methods when he founded Apple, he was also captivated by the simplicity and quality of Japanese porcelain in Kyoto.

It was not, however, an artisan from Kyoto who won Steve Jobs's devotion, but rather a *takumi* from Toyama named Yukio Shakunaga, who used a technique called *Etchu Seto-yaki*, known by only a few.

On a visit to Kyoto, Jobs heard of an exhibition of Shakunaga's work. He immediately understood that there was something special about Shakunaga's porcelain. As a matter of fact, he bought several cups, vases, and plates, and went back to the show three times that week.

Jobs returned to Kyoto several times over the course of his life in search of inspiration, and ended up meeting Shakunaga in person. It is said that Jobs had many questions for him—almost all of them about the fabrication process and the type of porcelain he used.

Shakunaga explained that he used white porcelain he extracted himself from mountains in the Toyama prefecture, making him the only artist of his ilk familiar with the fabrication process of porcelain objects from their origins in the mountains to their final form—an authentic *takumi*.

Jobs was so impressed that he considered going to Toyama to see the mountain where Shakunaga got his porcelain, but thought better of it when he heard that it was more than four hours by train from Kyoto.

In an interview after Jobs's death, Shakunaga said he was very proud that his work had been appreciated by the man who created the iPhone. He added that Jobs's last purchase from him had been a set of twelve teacups. Jobs had asked for something special, "a new style." To satisfy this request, Shakunaga made 150 teacups in the process of testing out new ideas. Of these, he chose the twelve best and sent them to the Jobs family.

Ever since his first trip to Japan, Jobs was fascinated and inspired by the country's artisans, engineers (especially at Sony), philosophy (especially Zen), and cuisine (especially sushi).[7]

Sophisticated simplicity

What do Japanese artisans, engineers, Zen philosophy, and cuisine have in common? Simplicity and attention to detail. It is not a lazy simplicity but a sophisticated one that searches out new frontiers, always taking the object, the body and mind, or the cuisine to the next level, according to one's *ikigai*.

As Csikszentmihalyi would say, the key is always having a meaningful challenge to overcome in order to maintain flow.

The documentary *Jiro Dreams of Sushi* gives us another example of a *takumi*, this time in the kitchen. Its protagonist has been making sushi every day for more than eighty years, and owns a small sushi restaurant near the Ginza subway station in Tokyo. He and his son go every day to the famous Tsukiji fish market and choose the best fish to bring back to the restaurant.

In the documentary, we see one of Jiro's apprentices learning to make tamago (a thin, slightly sweet omelet). No matter how hard he tries, he can't get Jiro's approval. He keeps practicing for years until he finally does.

Why does the apprentice refuse to give up? Doesn't he get bored cooking eggs every day? No, because making sushi is his *ikigai*, too.

Both Jiro and his son are culinary artists. They don't get bored when they cook—they achieve a state of flow. They enjoy themselves completely when they are in the kitchen; that is their happiness, their *ikigai*. They've learned to take pleasure in their work, to lose their sense of time.

Beyond the close relationship between father and son, which helps them keep the challenge going each day, they also work in a quiet, peaceful environment that allows them to concentrate. Even after receiving a three-star rating from Michelin, they never considered opening other locations or expanding the business. They serve just ten patrons at a time at the bar of their small restaurant. Jiro's family isn't looking to make money; instead they value good working conditions and creating an environment in which they can flow while making the best sushi in the world.

Jiro, like Yukio Shakunaga, begins his work at "the source." He goes to the fish market to find the best tuna; Shakunaga goes to the mountains to find the best porcelain. When they get down to work, both become one with the object they are creating. This unity with the object that they reach in a state of flow takes on special meaning in Japan, where, according to Shintoism, forests, trees, and objects have a *kami* (spirit or god) within them.

When someone—whether an artist, an engineer, or a chef—sets out to create something, his or her responsibility is to use nature to give it "life" while respecting that nature at every moment. During this process, the artisan becomes one with the object and flows with it. An ironworker would say that metal has a life of its own, just as someone making ceramics would say that the clay does. The Japanese are skilled at bringing nature and technology together: not man versus nature, but rather a union of the two.

The purity of Ghibli

There are those who say that the Shinto value of being connected with nature is vanishing. One of the harshest critics of this loss is another artist with a clearly defined *ikigai*: Hayao Miyazaki, the director of the animated films produced by Studio Ghibli.

In nearly all his films we see humans, technology, fantasy, and nature in a state of conflict—and, in the end, coming together. One of the most poignant metaphors in his film *Spirited Away* is an obese spirit covered in trash that represents the pollution of the rivers.

In Miyazaki's films, forests have personalities, trees have feelings, and robots befriend birds. Considered a national treasure by the Japanese government, Miyazaki is an artist capable of becoming completely absorbed in his art. He uses a cell phone from the late 1990s, and he makes his entire team draw by hand. He "directs" his films by rendering on paper even the tiniest detail, achieving flow by drawing, not by using a computer. Thanks to this obsession on the director's part, Studio Ghibli is one of the only studios in the world where almost the entire production process is carried out using traditional techniques.

Those who have visited Studio Ghibli know that it is fairly typical, on a given Sunday to see a solitary individual tucked away in a corner, hard at work—a man in simple clothes who will greet them with an *ohayo* (hello) without looking up.

Miyazaki is so passionate about his work that he spends many Sundays in the studio, enjoying the state of flow, putting his *ikigai* above all else. Visitors know that under no circumstances is one to bother Miyazaki, who is known for his quick temper—especially if he is interrupted while drawing.

In 2013, Miyazaki announced he was going to retire. To commemorate his retirement, the television station NHK made a documentary showing him in his last days at work. He is drawing in nearly every scene of the film. In one scene, several of his colleagues are seen coming out of a meeting, and there he is, drawing in a corner, paying no attention to them. In another scene, he is shown walking to work on December 30 (a national holiday in Japan) and opening the doors of Studio Ghibli so he can spend the day there, drawing alone.

Miyazaki can't stop drawing. The day after his "retirement," instead of going on vacation or staying at home, he went to Studio Ghibli and sat down to draw. His colleagues put on their best poker faces, not knowing what to say. One year later, he announced he wouldn't make any more feature films but that he would keep on drawing until the day he died.

Can someone really retire if he is passionate about what he does?

The recluses

It is not only the Japanese who have this capacity; there are artists and scientists all over the world with strong, clear *ikigais*. They do what they love until their dying day.

The last thing Einstein wrote before closing his eyes forever was a formula that attempted to unite all the forces of the universe in a single theory. When he died, he was still doing what he loved. If he hadn't been a physicist, he said, he would have been happy as a musician. When he wasn't focused on physics or mathematics, he enjoyed playing the violin. Reaching a state of flow while working on his formulas or playing music, his two *ikigais*, brought him endless pleasure.

Many such artists might seem misanthropic or reclusive,

but what they are really doing is protecting the time that brings them happiness, sometimes at the expense of other aspects of their lives. They are outliers who apply the principles of flow to their lives to an extreme.

Another example of this kind of artist is the novelist Haruki Murakami. He sees only a close circle of friends, and appears in public in Japan only once every few years.

Artists know how important it is to protect their space, control their environment, and be free of distractions if they want to flow with their *ikigai*.

Microflow: Enjoying mundane tasks

But what happens when we have to, say, do the laundry, mow the lawn, or attend to paperwork? Is there a way to make these mundane tasks enjoyable?

Near the Shinjuku subway station, in one of the neural centers of Tokyo, there is a supermarket that still employs elevator operators. The elevators are fairly standard and could easily be operated by the customers, but the store prefers to provide the service of someone holding the door open for you, pushing the button for your floor, and bowing as you exit.

If you ask around, you'll learn that there is one elevator operator who has been doing the same job since 2004. She is always smiling and enthusiastic about her work. How is she able to enjoy such a job? Doesn't she get bored doing something so repetitive?

On closer inspection, it becomes clear that the elevator operator is not just pushing buttons but is instead performing a whole sequence of movements. She begins by greeting the customers with a songlike salutation followed by a bow and a welcoming wave of the hand. Then she presses the elevator button with a graceful movement, as though she is a geisha offering a client a cup of tea.

Csikszentmihalyi calls this *microflow*.

We've all been bored in a class or at a conference and started doodling to keep ourselves entertained. Or whistled while painting a wall. If we're not truly being challenged, we get bored and add a layer of complexity to amuse ourselves. Our ability to turn routine tasks into moments of microflow, into something we enjoy, is key to our being happy, since we all have to do such tasks.

Even Bill Gates washes the dishes every night. He says he enjoys it—that it helps him relax and clear his mind, and that he tries to do it a little better each day, following an established order or set of rules he's made for himself: plates first, forks second, and so on.

It's one of his daily moments of microflow.

Richard Feynman, one of the most important physicists of all time, also took pleasure in routine tasks. W. Daniel Hillis, one of the founders of the supercomputer manufacturer Thinking Machines, hired Feynman to work on the development of a computer that could handle parallel processing when he was already world famous. He says Feynman showed up on his first day of work and said, "OK, boss, what's my assignment?" They didn't have anything prepared, so they asked him to work on a certain mathematical problem. He immediately realized they were giving him an irrelevant task to keep him busy and said, "That sounds like a bunch of baloney—give me something real to do."

So they sent him to a nearby shop to buy office supplies, and he completed his assignment with a smile on his face. When he didn't have something important to do or needed to rest his mind, Feynman dedicated himself to microflowing— say, painting the office walls.

Weeks later, after visiting the Thinking Machines offices a group of investors declared, "You have a Nobel laureate in there painting walls and soldering circuits."[8]

Instant vacations: Getting there through meditation

Training the mind can get us to a place of flow more quickly. Meditation is one way to exercise our mental muscles.

There are many types of meditation, but they all have the

same objective: calming the mind, observing our thoughts and emotions, and centering our focus on a single object.

The basic practice involves sitting with a straight back and focusing on your breath. Anyone can do it, and you feel a difference after just one session. By fixing your attention on the air moving in and out of your nose, you can slow the torrent of thoughts and clear your mental horizons.

The Archer's Secret

The winner of the 1988 Olympic gold medal for archery was a seventeen-year-old woman from South Korea. When asked how she prepared, she replied that the most important part of her training was meditating for two hours each day.

If we want to get better at reaching a state of flow, meditation is an excellent antidote to our smartphones and their notifications constantly clamoring for our attention.

One of the most common mistakes among people starting to meditate is worrying about doing it "right," achieving absolute mental silence, or reaching "nirvana." The most important thing is to focus on the journey.

Since the mind is a constant swirl of thoughts, ideas, and emotions, slowing down the "centrifuge"—even for just a few seconds—can help us feel more rested and leave us with a sense of clarity.

In fact, one of the things we learn in the practice of meditation is not to worry about anything that flits across our mental screen. The idea of killing our boss might flash into our mind, but we simply label it as a thought and let it pass like a cloud, without judging or rejecting it. It is only a thought—one of the sixty thousand we have every day, according to some experts.

Meditation generates alpha and theta brain waves. For those experienced in meditation, these waves appear right away, while it might take a half hour for a beginner to experience them. These relaxing brain waves are the ones that are activated right before we fall asleep, as we lie in the sun, or right after taking a hot bath.

We all carry a spa with us everywhere we go. It's just a matter of knowing how to get in—something anyone can do, with a bit of practice.

Humans as ritualistic beings

Life is inherently ritualistic. We could argue that humans naturally follow rituals that keep us busy. In some modern cultures, we have been forced out of our ritualistic lives to pursue goal after goal in order to be seen as successful. But throughout history, humans have always been busy. We were hunting, cooking, farming, exploring, and raising families—activities that were structured as rituals to keep us busy throughout our days.

But in an unusual way, rituals still permeate daily life and business practices in modern Japan. The main religions in Japan—Confucianism, Buddhism, and Shintoism—are all ones in which the rituals are more important than absolute rules.

When doing business in Japan, process, manners, and how you work on something is more important than the final results. Whether this is good or bad for the economy is beyond the scope of this book. What is indisputable, though, is that finding flow in a "ritualistic workplace" is much easier than in one in which we are continually stressed out trying to achieve unclear goals set by our bosses.

Rituals give us clear rules and objectives, which help us enter a state of flow. When we have only a big goal in front of us, we might feel lost or overwhelmed by it; rituals help us by giving us the process, the *substeps*, on the path to achieving a goal. When confronted with a big goal, try to break it down into parts and then attack each part one by one.

Focus on enjoying your daily rituals, using them as tools to enter a state of flow. Don't worry about the outcome—it will come naturally. Happiness is in the doing, not in the result. As a rule of thumb, remind yourself: "Rituals over goals."

The happiest people are not the ones who achieve the most. They are the ones who spend more time than others in a state of flow.

Using flow to find your *ikigai*

After reading this chapter you should have a better idea of which activities in your life make you enter flow. Write all of them on a piece of paper, then ask yourself these questions: What do the activities that drive you to flow have in common? Why do those activities drive you to flow? For example, are all the activities you most like doing ones that you practice alone or with other people? Do you flow more when doing things that require you to move your body or just to think?

In the answers to these questions you might find the underlying *ikigai* that drives your life. If you don't, then keep searching by going deeper into what you like by spending more of your time in the activities that make you flow. Also, try new things that are not on the list of what makes you flow but that are similar and that you are curious about. For example, if photography is something that drives you into flow, you could also try painting; you might even like it more! Or if you love snowboarding and have never tried surfing . . .

Flow is mysterious. It is like a muscle: the more you train it, the more you will flow, and the closer you will be to your *ikigai*.

V

MASTERS OF LONGEVITY

Words of wisdom
from the longest-living
people in the world

WHEN WE STARTED working on this book, we didn't want to just research the factors that contribute to a long and happy life; we wanted to hear from the true masters of this art.

The interviews we conducted in Okinawa merit their own chapter, but in the section that precedes it we have provided an overview of the life philosophies of a few international champions of longevity. We're talking about supercentenarians—people who live to 110 years of age or more.

The term was coined in 1970 by Norris McWhirter, editor of *The Guinness Book of World Records*. Its use became more widespread in the 1990s, after it appeared in William Strauss and Neil Howe's *Generations*. Today there are an estimated 300 to 450 supercentenarians in the world, although the age of only around 75 of them has been confirmed. They aren't superheroes, but we could see them as such for having spent far more time on this planet than the average life expectancy would predict.

Given the rise in life expectancy around the world, the number of supercentenarians might also increase. A healthy and purposeful life could help us join their ranks.

Let's take a look at what a few of them have to say.

Misao Okawa (117)
"Eat and sleep, and you'll live a long time. You have to learn to relax."

According to the Gerontology Research Group, until April 2015, the oldest living person in the world was Misao Okawa, who passed away in a care facility in Osaka, Japan, after living for 117 years and 27 days.

The daughter of a textile merchant, she was born in 1898, when Spain lost its colonies in Cuba and the Philippines, and the United States annexed Hawaii and launched Pepsi-Cola. Until she was 110, this woman—who lived in three different centuries—cared for herself unassisted.

When specialists asked about her self-care routine, Misao answered simply, "Eating sushi and sleeping," to which we should add, having a tremendous thirst for life. When they inquired about her secret for longevity, she answered with a smile, "I ask myself the same thing."[1]

Proof that Japan continues to be a factory of long life: In July of the same year Sakari Momoi passed away at 112 years and 150 days old. At the time he was the oldest man in the world, though he was younger than fifty-seven women.

María Capovilla (116)
"I've never eaten meat in my life."

Born in Ecuador in 1889, María Capovilla was recognized by Guinness as the world's oldest person. She died of pneumonia in 2006, at 116 years and 347 days old, leaving behind three children, twelve grandchildren, and twenty great- and great-great-grandchildren.

She gave one of her last interviews at age 107, sharing her memories and her thoughts:

I'm happy, and I give thanks to God, who keeps me going. I never thought I'd live so long, I thought I'd die long ago. My husband, Antonio Capovilla, was the captain of a ship. He passed away at 84. We had two daughters and a son, and now I have many grandchildren and great-grandchildren.

Things were better, back in the old days. People behaved better. We used to dance, but we were more restrained; there was this one song I loved dancing to: "María" by Luis Alarcón. I still remember most of the words. I also remember many prayers, and say them every day.

I like the waltz, and can still dance it. I also still make crafts, I still do some of the things I did when I was in school.[2]

When she had finished recalling her past, she began to dance—one of her great passions—with an energy that made her seem decades younger.

When asked about her secret for longevity, she responded simply, "I don't know what the secret to long life is. The only thing I do is I've never eaten meat in my life. I attribute it to that."

Jeanne Calment (122)
"Everything's fine."

Born in Arles, France, in February 1875, Jeanne Calment lived until August 4, 1997, making her, at 122, the oldest person of verified age in history. She jokingly said that she "competed with Methuselah," and there is no question that she broke numerous records as she went on celebrating birthdays.

She died of natural causes at the end of a happy life during which she denied herself almost nothing. She rode a bicycle until she turned 100. She lived on her own until 110, when she agreed to move into a nursing home after accidentally starting a small fire in her apartment. She stopped smoking at 120, when her cataracts started making it hard for her to bring a cigarette to her lips.

One of her secrets may have been her sense of humor. As

she said on her 120th birthday, "I see badly, I hear badly, and I feel bad, but everything's fine."[3]

Walter Breuning (114)
"If you keep your mind and body busy, you'll be around a long time."

Born in Minnesota in 1896, Walter Breuning was able to see three centuries in his lifetime. He died in Montana in 2011, from natural causes; he'd had two wives and a fifty-year career on the railroad. At eighty-three he retired to an assisted living center in Montana, where he remained until his death. He is the second-oldest man (of verified age) ever born in the United States.

He gave many interviews in his final years, insisting that his longevity stemmed from, among other things, his habit of eating only two meals per day and working for as many years as he could. "Your mind and your body. You keep both busy," he said on his 112th birthday, "you'll be here a long time." Back then, he was still exercising every day.

Among Breuning's other secrets: He had a habit of helping others, and he wasn't afraid of dying. As he declared in a 2010 interview with the Associated Press, "We're all going to die. Some people are scared of dying. Never be afraid to die. Because you're born to die."[4]

Before passing away in 2011, he is said to have told a pastor that he'd made a deal with God: If he wasn't going to get better, it was time to go.

Alexander Imich (111)
"I just haven't died yet."

Born in Poland in 1903, Alexander Imich was a chemist and parapsychologist residing in the United States who, after the death of his predecessor in 2014, became the oldest man of authenticated age in the world. Imich himself died shortly thereafter, in June of that year, leaving behind a long life rich with experiences.

Imich attributed his longevity to, among other things, never drinking alcohol. "It's not as though I'd won the Nobel Prize," he said upon being declared the world's oldest man. "I never thought I'd get to be so old." When asked about his secret to living so long, his answer was "I don't know. I just haven't died yet."[5]

Ikigai artists
The secret to long life, however, is not held by supercentenarians alone. There are many people of advanced age who, though they haven't made it into *Guinness World Records*, offer us

inspiration and ideas for bringing energy and meaning to our lives.

Artists, for example, who carry the torch of their *ikigai* instead of retiring, have this power.

Art, in all its forms, is an *ikigai* that can bring happiness and purpose to our days. Enjoying or creating beauty is free, and something all human beings have access to.

Hokusai, the Japanese artist who made woodblock prints in the ukiyo-e style and lived for 88 years, from the mid-eighteenth to the mid-nineteenth century, added this postscript to the first edition of his *One Hundred Views of Mount Fuji*:[6]

> All that I have produced before the age of 70 is not worth being counted. It is at the age of 73 that I have somewhat begun to understand the structure of true nature, of animals and grasses, and trees and birds, and fishes and insects; consequently at 80 years of age I shall have made still more progress; at 90 I hope to have penetrated into the mystery of things; at 100 years of age I should have reached decidedly a marvelous degree, and when I shall be 110, all that I do, every point and every line, shall be instinct with life.

In the pages that follow, we've collected some of the most inspirational words from artists interviewed by Camille Sweeney for the *New York Times*.[7] Of those still living, none have retired, and all still enjoy their passion, which they plan to pursue until their final breath, demonstrating that when you have a clear purpose, no one can stop you.

The actor Christopher Plummer, still working at eighty-six, reveals a dark desire shared by many who love the profession: "We want to drop dead onstage. That would be a nice theatrical way to go."[8]

Osamu Tezuka, the father of modern Japanese manga, shared this feeling. Before he died in 1989, his last words as he drew one final cartoon were "Please, just let me work!"[9]

The eighty-six-year-old filmmaker Frederick Wiseman declared on a stroll through Paris that he likes to work, which is why he does it with such intensity. "Everybody complains about their aches and pains and all that, but my friends are either dead or are still working," he said.[10]

Carmen Herrera, a painter who just entered her one hundredth year, sold her first canvas at age eighty-nine. Today her work is in the permanent collections of the Tate Modern and the Museum of Modern Art. When asked how she viewed her future, she responded, "I am always waiting to finish the next thing. Absurd, I know. I go day by day."[11]

Never Stop Learning

"You may grow old and trembling in your anatomies, you may lie awake at night listening to the disorder of your veins, you may miss your only love, you may see the world about you devastated by evil lunatics, or know your honour trampled in the sewers of baser minds. There is only one thing for it then—to learn. Learn why the world wags and what wags it. That is the only thing which the mind can never exhaust, never alienate, never be tortured by, never fear or distrust, and never dream of regretting."

—T. H. White, *The Once and Future King*

For his part, naturalist and author Edward O. Wilson asserted, "I feel I have enough experience to join those who are addressing big questions. About ten years ago, when I began reading and thinking more broadly about the questions of what are we, where did we come from and where are we going, I was astonished at how little this was being done."[12]

Ellsworth Kelly, an artist who passed away in 2015 at the age of ninety-two, assured us that the idea that we lose our faculties with age is, in part, a myth, because instead we develop a greater clarity and capacity for observation. "It's one thing about getting older, you see more. . . . Every day I'm continuing to see new things. That's why there are new paintings."[13]

At eighty-six, the architect Frank Gehry reminds us that some buildings can take seven years "from the time you're hired until you're finished,"[14] a fact that favors a patient attitude with regard to the passage of time. The man responsible for the Guggenheim Museum Bilbao, however, knows how to live in the here and now: "You stay in your time. You don't go backward. I think if you relate to the time you're in, you keep your eyes and ears open, read the paper, see what's going on, stay curious about everything, you will automatically be in your time."[15]

Longevity in Japan

Because of its robust civil registry, many of those verified as having lived the longest are found in the United States; however, there are many centenarians living in remote villages in other countries. A peaceful life in the countryside seems pretty common among people who have watched a century pass.

Without question, the international superstar of longevity is Japan, which has the highest life expectancy of any country in the world. In addition to a healthy diet, which we will explore in detail, and an integrated health care system in which people go to the doctor for regular checkups to prevent disease, longevity in Japan is closely tied to its culture, as we will see later on.

The sense of community, and the fact that Japanese people make an effort to stay active until the very end, are key elements of their secret to long life.

If you want to stay busy even when there's no need to work, there has to be an *ikigai* on your horizon, a purpose that guides you throughout your life and pushes you to make things of beauty and utility for the community and yourself.

VI

LESSONS FROM JAPAN'S CENTENARIANS

Traditions and proverbs for happiness and longevity

To GET TO Ogimi, we had to fly nearly three hours from Tokyo to Naha, the capital of Okinawa. Several months earlier we had contacted the town council of a place known as the Village of Longevity to explain the purpose of our trip and our intention to interview the oldest members of the community. After numerous conversations, we finally got the help we were looking for and were able to rent a house just outside the town.

One year after starting this project, we found ourselves on the doorstep of some of the longest-living people in the world.

We realized right away that time seems to have stopped there, as though the entire town were living in an endless here and now.

Arriving in Ogimi

After two hours on the road from Naha, we're finally able to stop worrying about the traffic. To our left are the sea and an empty stretch of beach; to our right, the mountainous jungle of Okinawa's Yanbaru forests.

Once Route 58 passes Nago, where Orion beer—the pride of Okinawa—is made, it skirts the coast until it reaches Ogimi. Every now and then a few little houses and stores crop up in the narrow stretch of land between the road and the base of the mountain.

We pass small clusters of houses scattered here and there

as we enter the municipality of Ogimi, but the town doesn't really seem to have a center. Our GPS finally guides us to our destination: the Center for the Support and Promotion of Well-Being, housed in an unattractive cinderblock building right off the highway.

We go in through the back door, where a man named Taira is waiting for us. Beside him is a petite, cheerful woman who introduces herself as Yuki. Two other women immediately get up from desks and show us to a conference room. They serve us each a cup of green tea and a few *shikuwasa*, a small citrus fruit that packs a big nutritional punch, as we will see later on.

Taira sits down across from us in his formal suit and opens up a large planner and a three-ring binder. Yuki sits next to him. The binder contains a list of all the town's residents, organized by age and "club," or *moai*. Taira points out that these groups of people who help one another are characteristic of Ogimi. The *moai* are not organized around any concrete objective; they function more like a family. Taira also tells us that volunteer work, rather than money, drives much of what happens in Ogimi. Everyone offers to pitch in, and the local government takes care of assigning tasks. This way, everyone can be useful and feels like a part of the community.

Ogimi is the penultimate town before Cape Hedo, the northernmost point of the largest island in the archipelago.

From the top of one of Ogimi's mountains, we're able to

look down over the whole town. Almost everything is the green of the Yanbaru jungle, making us wonder where the nearly thirty-two hundred residents are hiding. We can see a few houses, but they're scattered in little clusters near the sea or in small valleys accessible by side roads.

Communal life

We're invited to eat in one of Ogimi's few restaurants, but when we arrive the only three tables are already reserved.

"Don't worry, we'll go to Churaumi instead. It never fills up," says Yuki, walking back to her car.

She's still driving at age eighty-eight, and takes great pride in that. Her copilot is ninety-nine, and has also decided to spend the day with us. We have to drive fast to keep up with them on a highway that is sometimes more dirt than asphalt. Finally reaching the other end of the jungle, we can at last sit down to eat.

"I don't really go to restaurants," Yuki says as we take our seats. "Almost everything I eat comes from my vegetable garden, and I buy my fish from Tanaka, who's been my friend forever."

The restaurant is right by the sea and seems like something from the planet Tatooine, from *Star Wars*. The menu boasts in large letters that it serves "slow food" prepared with organic vegetables grown in the town.

"But really," Yuki continues, "food is the least important thing." She is extroverted, and rather pretty. She likes to talk about her role as the director of several associations run by the local government.

"Food won't help you live longer," she says, bringing to her lips a bite of the diminutive confection that followed our meal. "The secret is smiling and having a good time."

There are no bars and only a few restaurants in Ogimi, but those who live there enjoy a rich social life that revolves around community centers. The town is divided into seventeen neighborhoods, and each one has a president and several people in charge of things like culture, festivals, social activities, and longevity.

Residents pay close attention to this last category.

We're invited to the community center of one of the seventeen neighborhoods. It is an old building right next to one of the mountains of the Yanbaru jungle, home to bunagaya, the town's iconic sprites.

The Bunagaya Spirits of the Yanbaru Jungle

Bunagaya are magical creatures that inhabit the Yanbaru jungle near Ogimi and its surrounding towns. They manifest as children with long red hair, and like to hide in the jungle's gajumaru (banyan) trees and go fishing on the beach.

Many of Okinawa's stories and fables are about bunagaya sprites. They are mischievous, playful, and unpredictable. Locals say that the bunagaya love the mountains, rivers, sea, trees, earth, wind, and animals, and that if you want to befriend them, you have to show respect for nature.

A birthday party

When we arrive at the neighborhood's community center, we're greeted by a group of about twenty people who proudly proclaim, "The youngest among us is eighty-three!"

We conduct our interviews at a large table while drinking green tea. When we finish, we're brought to an event space, where we celebrate the birthdays of three members of the group. One woman is turning ninety-nine, another ninety-four, and one "young man" has just reached eighty-nine.

We sing a few songs popular in the village and finish up with "Happy Birthday" in English. The woman turning ninety-nine blows out the candles and thanks everyone for coming to her party. We eat homemade *shikuwasa* cake and end up dancing and celebrating as though it were the birthday of a twentysomething.

It's the first party, but not the last, that we'll attend during our week in the village. We'll also do karaoke with a group of seniors who sing better than we do, and attend a traditional festival with local bands, dancers, and food stands at the foot of a mountain.

Celebrate each day, together

Celebrations seem to be an essential part of life in Ogimi.

We're invited to watch a game of gateball, one of the most popular sports among Okinawa's older residents. It involves hitting a ball with a mallet-like stick. It is a low-impact sport that can be played anywhere, and is a good excuse to move around and have fun as a group. The residents hold local competitions, and there is no age limit for participants.

We participate in the weekly game and lose to a woman who recently turned 104. Everyone cheers, and the defeated look on our faces elicits laughter.

In addition to playing and celebrating as a community, spirituality is also essential to the happiness of the village's residents.

The gods of Okinawa

The main religion in Okinawa is known as Ryukyu Shinto. *Ryukyu* is the original name of the Okinawa archipelago, and *Shinto* means "the path of the gods."[1] Ryukyu Shinto combines elements of Chinese Taoism, Confucianism, Buddhism, and Shintoism with shamanistic and animistic elements.

According to this ancient faith, the world is populated by an infinite number of spirits divided into several types: spirits of the home, of the forest, of the trees, and of the mountains. It is important to appease these spirits through rituals and festivals, and by consecrating sacred grounds.

Okinawa is full of sacred jungles and forests, where many of the two main kinds of temples are found: the *utaki* and the *uganju*. We visited an *uganju*, or small, open-air temple adorned with incense and coins, next to a waterfall in Ogimi. The *utaki* is a collection of stones where people go to pray and where, supposedly, spirits gather.

In Okinawa's religious practice, women are considered spiritually superior to men, whereas the opposite is true of traditional Shintoism in the rest of Japan. *Yuta* are women chosen as mediums by their communities to make contact with the spirit realm through traditional rites.

Ancestor worship is another important feature of spiritual

practice in Okinawa, and in Japan in general. The home of each generation's firstborn usually contains a *butsudan*, or small altar, used to pray for and make offerings to the family's ancestors.

Mabui

Every person has an essence, or *mabui*. This *mabui* is our spirit and the source of our life force. It is immortal and makes us who we are.

Sometimes, the *mabui* of someone who has died is trapped in the body of a living person. This situation requires a separation ritual to free the *mabui* of the deceased; it often happens when a person dies suddenly—especially at a young age—and his or her *mabui* does not want to move on to the realm of the dead.

A *mabui* can also be passed from person to person by physical contact. A grandmother who leaves her granddaughter a ring transfers a part of her *mabui* to her. Photographs can also be a medium for passing *mabui* among people.

The older, the stronger

Looking back, our days in Ogimi were intense but relaxed—sort of like the lifestyle of the locals, who always seemed to be busy with important tasks but who, upon closer inspection, did everything with a sense of calm. They were always pursuing their *ikigai*, but they were never in a rush.

Not only did they seem to be happily busy, but we also noticed that they followed the other principles for happiness that Washington Burnap stated two hundred years ago: "The grand essentials to happiness in this life are something to do, something to love, and something to hope for."[2]

On our last day, we went to buy gifts at a small market at the edge of town. The only things sold there are local vegetables, green tea, and *shikuwasa* juice, along with bottles of water from a spring hidden in the Yanbaru forests, bearing labels that read "Longevity Water."

We bought ourselves some of this Longevity Water and drank it in the parking lot, looking out over the sea and hoping that the little bottles that promised a magic elixir would bring us health and long life, and would help us find our own *ikigai*. Then we took a photo with a statue of a bunagaya, and walked up to it one last time to read the inscription:

A Declaration from the Town Where People Live Longest
At 80 I am still a child.
When I come to see you at 90,
send me away to wait until I'm 100.
The older, the stronger;

let us not depend too much on our children as we age.
If you seek long life and health, you are welcome in
    our village,
where you will be blessed by nature,
and together we will discover the secret to longevity.

April 23, 1993
Ogimi Federation of Senior Citizen Clubs

The interviews

Over the course of a week we conducted a total of one hundred interviews, asking the eldest members of the community about their life philosophy, their *ikigai*, and the secrets to longevity. We filmed these conversations with two cameras for use in a little documentary, and chose a few especially meaningful and inspiring statements to include in this section of the book.

I. Don't worry

"The secret to a long life is not to worry. And to keep your heart young—don't let it grow old. Open your heart to people with a nice smile on your face. If you smile and open your heart, your grandchildren and everyone else will want to see you."

"The best way to avoid anxiety is to go out in the street and say hello to people. I do it every day. I go out there and say, 'Hello!'

and 'See you later!' Then I go home and care for my vegetable garden. In the afternoon, I spend time with friends."

"Here, everyone gets along. We try not to cause problems. Spending time together and having fun is the only thing that matters."

2. Cultivate good habits

"I feel joy every morning waking up at six and opening the curtains to look out at my garden, where I grow my own vegetables. I go right outside to check on my tomatoes, my mandarin oranges . . . I love the sight of them—it relaxes me. After an hour in the garden I go back inside and make breakfast."

"I plant my own vegetables and cook them myself. That's my *ikigai*."

"The key to staying sharp in old age is in your fingers. From your fingers to your brain, and back again. If you keep your fingers busy, you'll live to see one hundred."

"I get up at four every day. I set my alarm for that time, have a cup of coffee, and do a little exercise, lifting my arms. That gives me energy for the rest of the day."

"I eat a bit of everything; I think that's the secret. I like variety in what I eat; I think it tastes better."

"Working. If you don't work, your body breaks down."

"When I wake up, I go to the *butsudan* and light incense. You have to keep your ancestors in mind. It's the first thing I do every morning."

"I wake up every day at the same time, early, and spend the morning in my vegetable garden. I go dancing with my friends once a week."

"I do exercise every day, and every morning I go for a little walk."

"I never forget to do my taiso exercises when I get up."

"Eating vegetables—it helps you live longer."

"To live a long time you need to do three things: exercise to stay healthy, eat well, and spend time with people."

3. Nurture your friendships every day

"Getting together with my friends is my most important *iki-gai*. We all get together here and talk—it's very important. I always know I'll see them all here tomorrow, and that's one of my favorite things in life."

"My main hobby is getting together with friends and neighbors."

"Talking each day with the people you love, that's the secret to a long life."

"I say, 'Hello!' and 'See you later!' to the children on their way to school, and wave at everyone who goes by me in their car. 'Drive safely!' I say. Between 7:20 a.m. and 8:15 a.m., I'm outside on my feet the whole time, saying hello to people. Once everyone's gone, I go back inside."

"Chatting and drinking tea with my neighbors. That's the best thing in life. And singing together."

"I wake up at five every morning, leave the house, and walk to the sea. Then I go to a friend's house and we have tea together. That's the secret to long life: getting together with people, and going from place to place."

4. Live an unhurried life

"My secret to a long life is always saying to myself, 'Slow down,' and 'Relax.' You live much longer if you're not in a hurry."

"I make things with wicker. That's my *ikigai*. The first thing I do when I wake up is pray. Then I do my exercises and eat breakfast. At seven I calmly start working on my wicker. When I get tired at five, I go visit my friends."

"Doing many different things every day. Always staying busy, but doing one thing at a time, without getting overwhelmed."

"The secret to long life is going to bed early, waking up early, and going for a walk. Living peacefully and enjoying the little things. Getting along with your friends. Spring, summer, fall, winter . . . enjoying each season, happily."

5. Be optimistic

"Every day I say to myself, 'Today will be full of health and energy. Live it to the fullest.'"

"I'm ninety-eight, but consider myself young. I still have so much to do."

"Laugh. Laughter is the most important thing. I laugh wherever I go."

"I'm going to live to be a hundred. Of course I am! It's a huge motivation for me."

"Dancing and singing with your grandchildren is the best thing in life."

"I feel very fortunate to have been born here. I give thanks for it every day."

"The most important thing in Ogimi, in life, is to keep smiling."

"I do volunteer work to give back to the village a bit of what it has given to me. For example, I use my car to help friends get to the hospital."

"There's no secret to it. The trick is just to live."

Keys to the Ogimi Lifestyle

- One hundred percent of the people we interviewed keep a vegetable garden, and most of them also have fields of tea, mangoes, *shikuwasa*, and so on.

- All belong to some form of neighborhood association, where they feel cared for as though by family.
- They celebrate all the time, even little things. Music, song, and dance are essential parts of daily life.
- They have an important purpose in life, or several. They have an *ikigai*, but they don't take it too seriously. They are relaxed and enjoy all that they do.
- They are very proud of their traditions and local culture.
- They are passionate about everything they do, however insignificant it might seem.
- Locals have a strong sense of *yuimaaru*—recognizing the connection between people. They help each other with everything from work in the fields (harvesting sugarcane or planting rice) to building houses and municipal projects. Our friend Miyagi, who ate dinner with us on our last night in town, told us that he was building a new home with the help of all his friends, and that we could stay there the next time we were in Ogimi.
- They are always busy, but they occupy themselves with tasks that allow them to relax. We didn't see a single old grandpa sitting on a bench doing nothing. They're always coming and going—to sing karaoke, visit with neighbors, or play a game of gateball.

VII

THE IKIGAI DIET

What the world's
longest-living people
eat and drink

ACCORDING TO THE World Health Organization, Japan has the highest life expectancy in the world: 85 years for men and 87.3 years for women. Moreover, it has the highest ratio of centenarians in the world: more than 520 for every million people (as of September 2016).

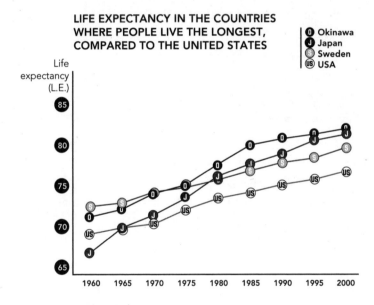

LIFE EXPECTANCY IN THE COUNTRIES WHERE PEOPLE LIVE THE LONGEST, COMPARED TO THE UNITED STATES

Okinawa
Japan
Sweden
USA

Source: World Health Organization, 1966; Japanese Ministry of Health, Labor and Welfare, 2004; U.S. Department of Health and Human Services/CDC, 2005

The above graphic, which compares life expectancy in Japan, its province Okinawa, Sweden, and the United States, shows that, while life expectancy in Japan is high overall, Okinawa exceeds the national average.

Okinawa is one of the areas in Japan that were most affected by World War II. As a result not only of conflicts on the battlefield but also of hunger and a lack of resources once the war ended, the average life expectancy was not very high during the 1940s and 1950s. As Okinawans recovered from the destruction, however, they came to be some of the country's longest-living citizens.

What secrets to long life do the Japanese hold? What is it about Okinawa that makes it the best of the best in terms of life expectancy?

Experts point out that, for one thing, Okinawa is the only province in Japan without trains. Its residents have to walk or cycle when not driving. It is also the only province that has managed to follow the Japanese government's recommendation of eating less than ten grams of salt per day.

Okinawa's miracle diet

The mortality rate from cardiovascular disease in Okinawa is the lowest in Japan, and diet almost certainly has a lot to do with this. It is no coincidence that the "Okinawa Diet" is so often discussed around the world at panels on nutrition.

The most concrete and widely cited data on diet in

Okinawa come from studies by Makoto Suzuki, a cardiologist at the University of the Ryukyus, who has published more than seven hundred scientific articles on nutrition and aging in Okinawa since 1970.

Bradley J. Willcox and D. Craig Willcox joined Makoto Suzuki's research team and published a book considered the bible on the subject, *The Okinawa Program*.[1] They reached the following conclusions:

- Locals eat a *wide variety of foods*, especially vegetables. Variety seems to be key. A study of Okinawa's centenarians showed that they ate 206 different foods, including spices, on a regular basis. They ate an average of eighteen different foods each day, a striking contrast to the nutritional poverty of our fast-food culture.
- *They eat at least five servings of fruits and vegetables every day.* At least seven types of fruits and vegetables are consumed by Okinawans on a daily basis. The easiest way to check if there is enough variety on your table is to make sure you're "eating the rainbow." A table featuring red peppers, carrots, spinach, cauliflower, and eggplant, for example, offers great color and variety. Vegetables, potatoes, legumes, and soy products such as tofu are the staples of an Okinawan's diet. More than 30 percent of their daily calories comes from vegetables.

- *Grains are the foundation of their diet.* Japanese people eat white rice every day, sometimes adding noodles. Rice is the primary food in Okinawa, as well.
- *They rarely eat sugar*, and if they do, it's cane sugar. We drove through several sugarcane fields every morning on our way to Ogimi, and even drank a glass of cane juice at Nakijin Castle. Beside the stall selling the juice was a sign describing the anticarcinogenic benefits of sugarcane.

In addition to these basic dietary principles, Okinawans eat fish an average of three times per week; unlike in other parts of Japan, the most frequently consumed meat is pork, though locals eat it only once or twice per week.

Along these lines, Makoto Suzuki's studies indicate the following:

- Okinawans consume, in general, one-third as much sugar as the rest of Japan's population, which means that sweets and chocolate are much less a part of their diet.
- They also eat practically half as much salt as the rest of Japan: 7 grams per day, compared to an average of 12.
- They consume fewer calories: an average of 1,785 per day, compared to 2,068 in the rest of Japan. In fact, low caloric intake is common among the five Blue Zones.

Hara hachi bu

This brings us back to the 80 percent rule we mentioned in the first chapter, a concept known in Japanese as *hara hachi bu*. It's easy to do: When you notice you're almost full but *could* have a little more . . . just stop eating!

One easy way to start applying the concept of *hara hachi bu* is to skip dessert. Or to reduce portion size. The idea is to still be a *little bit* hungry when you finish.

This is why portion size tends to be much smaller in Japan than in the West. Food isn't served as appetizers, main courses, and dessert. Instead, it's much more common to see everything presented at once on small plates: one with rice, another with vegetables, a bowl of miso soup, and something to snack on. Serving food on many small plates makes it easier to avoid eating too much, and facilitates the varied diet discussed at the beginning of this chapter.

Hara hachi bu is an ancient practice. The twelfth-century book on Zen Buddhism *Zazen Youjinki* recommends eating two-thirds as much as you might want to. Eating less than one might want is common among all Buddhist temples in the East. Perhaps Buddhism recognized the benefits of limiting caloric intake more than nine centuries ago.

So, eat less to live longer?

Few would challenge this idea. Without taking it to the extreme of malnutrition, of course, eating fewer calories than our bodies ask for seems to increase longevity. The key to staying healthy while consuming fewer calories is eating foods with a high nutritional value (especially "superfoods") and avoiding those that add to our overall caloric intake but offer little to no nutritional value.

The calorie restriction we've been discussing is one of the most effective ways to add years to your life. If the body regularly consumes enough, or too many, calories, it gets lethargic and starts to wear down, expending significant energy on digestion alone.

Another benefit of calorie restriction is that it reduces levels of IGF-1 (insulin-like growth factor 1) in the body. IGF-1 is a protein that plays a significant role in the aging process; it seems that one of the reasons humans and animals age is an excess of this protein in their blood.[2]

Whether calorie restriction will extend lifespan in humans is not yet known, but data increasingly indicate that moderate calorie restriction with adequate nutrition has a powerful protective effect against obesity, type 2 diabetes, inflammation, hypertension, and cardiovascular disease and reduces metabolic risk factors associated with cancer.[3]

An alternative to following the 80 percent rule on a daily basis is to fast for one or two days each week. The 5:2 (or fasting) diet recommends two days of fasting (consuming fewer than five hundred calories) every week and eating normally on the other five days.

Among its many benefits, fasting helps cleanse the digestive system and allows it to rest.

15 natural antioxidants found in the Okinawan diet

Antioxidants are molecules that slow the oxidation process in cells, neutralizing the free radicals that cause damage and accelerate aging. The antioxidant power of green tea, for example, is well known, and will be discussed later at greater length.

Because they are rich in antioxidants and are eaten nearly every day in the region, these fifteen foods are considered keys to Okinawan vitality:

- Tofu
- Miso
- Tuna
- Carrots
- Goya (bitter melon)
- Kombu (sea kelp)

- Cabbage
- Nori (seaweed)
- Onion
- Soy sprouts
- Hechima (cucumber-like gourd)
- Soybeans (boiled or raw)
- Sweet potato
- Peppers
- Sanpin-cha (jasmine tea)

Sanpin-cha: The reigning infusion in Okinawa

Okinawans drink more Sanpin-cha—a mix of green tea and jasmine flowers—than any other kind of tea. The closest approximation in the West would be the jasmine tea that usually comes from China. A 1988 study conducted by Hiroko Sho at the Okinawa Institute of Science and Technology indicates that jasmine tea reduces blood cholesterol levels.[4]

Sanpin-cha can be found in many different forms in Okinawa, and is even available in vending machines. In addition to all the antioxidant benefits of green tea, it boasts the benefits of jasmine, which include:

- Reducing the risk of heart attack
- Strengthening the immune system

- Helping relieve stress
- Lowering cholesterol

Okinawans drink an average of three cups of Sanpin-cha every day.

It might be hard to find exactly the same blend in the West, but we can drink jasmine tea, or even a high-quality green tea, instead.

The secrets of green tea

Green tea has been credited for centuries with significant medicinal properties. Recent studies have confirmed its many benefits, and have attested to the importance of this ancient plant in the longevity of those who drink it often.

Originally from China, where it has been consumed for millennia, green tea didn't make its way to the rest of the world until just a few centuries ago. Unlike other teas, and as a result of being air-dried without fermentation, it retains its active elements even after being dried and crumbled. It offers meaningful health benefits such as:

- Controlling cholesterol
- Lowering blood sugar levels
- Improving circulation

- Protection against the flu (vitamin C)
- Promoting bone health (fluoride)
- Protection against certain bacterial infections
- Protection against UV damage
- Cleansing and diuretic effects

White tea, with its high concentration of polyphenols, may be even more effective against aging. In fact, it is considered to be the natural product with the greatest antioxidant power in the world—to the extent that one cup of white tea might pack the same punch as about a dozen glasses of orange juice.

In summary: Drinking green or white tea every day can help us reduce the free radicals in our bodies, keeping us young longer.

The powerful *shikuwasa*

Shikuwasa is the citrus fruit par excellence of Okinawa, and Ogimi is its largest producer in all of Japan.

The fruit is extremely acidic: It is impossible to drink *shikuwasa* juice without diluting it first with water. Its taste is somewhere between that of a lime and a mandarin orange, to which it bears a family resemblance.

Shikuwasas also contain high levels of nobiletin, a flavonoid rich in antioxidants.

All citrus fruits—grapefruits, oranges, lemons—are high in nobiletin, but Okinawa's *shikuwasas* have *forty times as much* as oranges. Consuming nobiletin has been proven to protect us from arteriosclerosis, cancer, type 2 diabetes, and obesity in general.

Shikuwasas also contain vitamins C and B_1, beta carotene, and minerals. They are used in many traditional dishes and to add flavor to food, and are squeezed to make juice. While conducting research at the birthday parties of the town's "grandparents," we were served *shikuwasa* cake.

The Antioxidant Canon, for Westerners

In 2010 the UK's *Daily Mirror* published a list of foods recommended by experts to combat aging. Among these foods readily available in the West are:

- Vegetables such as broccoli and chard, for their high concentration of water, minerals, and fiber
- Oily fish such as salmon, mackerel, tuna, and sardines, for all the antioxidants in their fat
- Fruits such as citrus, strawberries, and apricots; they are an excellent source of vitamins and help eliminate toxins from the body

- Berries such as blueberries and goji berries; they are rich in phytochemical antioxidants
- Dried fruits, which contain vitamins and antioxidants, and give you energy
- Grains such as oats and wheat, which give you energy and contain minerals
- Olive oil, for its antioxidant effects that show in your skin
- Red wine, in moderation, for its antioxidant and vasodilatory properties

Foods that should be eliminated are refined sugar and grains, processed baked goods, and prepared foods, along with cow's milk and all its derivatives. Following this diet will help you feel younger and slow the process of premature aging.

VIII

**GENTLE MOVEMENTS,
LONGER LIFE**

Exercises from the East
that promote health and
longevity

STUDIES FROM THE Blue Zones suggest that the people who live longest are not the ones who do the most exercise but rather the ones who *move* the most.

When we visited Ogimi, the Village of Longevity, we discovered that even people over eighty and ninety years old are still highly active. They don't stay at home looking out the window or reading the newspaper. Ogimi's residents walk a lot, do karaoke with their neighbors, get up early in the morning, and, as soon as they've had breakfast—or even before— head outside to weed their gardens. They don't go to the gym or exercise intensely, but they almost never stop moving in the course of their daily routines.

As Easy as Getting out of Your Chair

"Metabolism slows down 90 percent after 30 minutes of sitting. The enzymes that move the bad fat from your arteries to your muscles, where it can get burned off, slow down. And after two hours, good cholesterol drops 20 percent. Just getting up for five minutes is going to get things going again. These things are so simple they're almost stupid," says Gavin Bradley[1] in a 2015 interview with Brigid Schulte for the *Washington Post*.[2] Bradley is one of the preeminent experts on the subject, and the director of an international organization dedicated to building awareness of how detrimental sitting all the time can be to our health.

If we live in a city, we might find it hard to move in natural and healthy ways every day, but we can turn to exercises that have proven for centuries to be good for the body.

The Eastern disciplines for bringing body, mind, and soul into balance have become quite popular in the West, but in their countries of origin they have been used for ages to promote health.

Yoga—originally from India, though very popular in Japan—and China's qigong and tai chi, among other disciplines, seek to create harmony between a person's body and mind so they can face the world with strength, joy, and serenity.

They are touted as elixirs of youth, and science has endorsed the claim.

These gentle exercises offer extraordinary health benefits, and are particularly appropriate for older individuals who have a harder time staying fit.

Tai chi has been shown, among other things, to slow the development of osteoporosis and Parkinson's disease, to increase circulation, and to improve muscle tone and flexibility. Its emotional benefits are just as important: It is a great shield against stress and depression.

You don't need to go to the gym for an hour every day or run marathons. As Japanese centenarians show us, all you need is to add movement to your day. Practicing any of these Eastern disciplines on a regular basis is a great way to do so. An added benefit is that they all have well-defined steps, and as we saw in chapter IV, disciplines with clear rules are good for flow. If you don't like any of these disciplines, feel free to choose a practice that you love and that makes you move.

In the following pages we'll take a look at some of the practices that promote health and longevity—but first, a little appetizer: a singularly Japanese exercise for starting your day.

Radio taiso

This morning warm-up has been around since before World War II. The "radio" part of its name is from when the instructions for each exercise were transmitted over the radio, but today people usually do these movements while tuned to a television channel or Internet video demonstrating the steps.

One of the main purposes of doing radio taiso is to promote a spirit of unity among participants. The exercises are always done in groups, usually in schools before the start of classes, and in businesses before the workday begins.

Statistics show that 30 percent of Japanese practice radio taiso for a few minutes every morning, but radio taiso is one thing that almost everyone we interviewed in Ogimi had in common. Even the residents of the nursing home we visited dedicated at least five minutes every day to it, though some did the exercises from their wheelchairs. We joined them on their daily practice and we felt refreshed for the rest of the day.

When these exercises are done in a group, it is usually on a sports field or in a large reception hall, and typically involves some kind of loudspeaker.

The exercises take five or ten minutes, depending on whether you do all or only some of them. They focus on dynamic stretching and increasing joint mobility. One of the most iconic radio taiso exercises consists of simply raising your arms above your head and then bringing them down in a circular motion. It is a tool to wake up the body, an easy mobility workout that is low in intensity and that focuses on exercising as many joints as possible.

It might seem basic, but in our modern lives, we can spend days without raising our arms above our ears. Think about it: our arms are down when using computers, when using smartphones, when reading books. One of the few times we raise our hands over our heads is when reaching for something in a cupboard or closet, while our ancestors were raising their hands over their heads all the time when gathering things from trees. Radio taiso helps us to practice all the basic movements of the body.

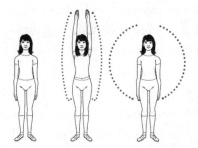

Basic version of the radio taiso exercises (5 minutes).

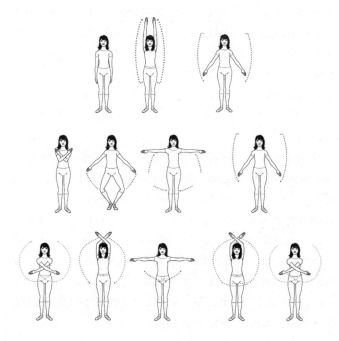

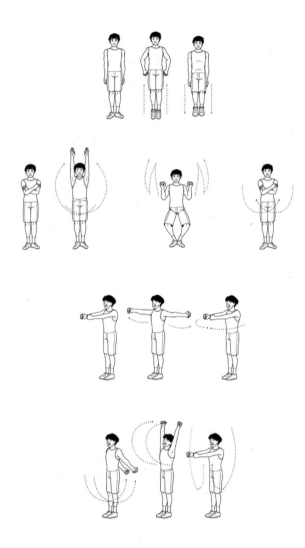

Yoga

Popular in Japan as well as in the West, yoga can be done by almost anyone. Some of its poses have even been adapted for pregnant women and practitioners with physical disabilities.

Yoga comes from India, where it was developed millennia ago to unite our mental and physical elements. The word *yoga* itself comes from the Sanskrit term for "yoke," which refers to the crosspiece that binds draft animals to one another and to the cart they're pulling. Yoga strives to unite body and mind in the same way, guiding us toward a healthy lifestyle in harmony with the world around us.

The main objectives of yoga are:

- To bring us closer to our (human) nature
- Mental and physical purification
- To bring us closer to the divine

Styles of yoga

Though all are oriented toward similar goals, there are many different types of yoga that vary according to the traditions and texts from which they were developed. The differences among them lie, as the masters say, in the path taken to the summit of our best self.

- *Jnana yoga*: the yoga of wisdom; the search for discipline and mental growth
- *Karma yoga*: focuses on action, on tasks and duties that benefit oneself and one's community
- *Bhakti yoga*: the yoga of devotion and surrender to the divine
- *Mantra yoga*: focuses on the recitation of mantras to reach a state of relaxation
- *Kundalini yoga*: combines diverse steps to reach the desired mental state
- *Raja yoga*: also known as the royal path; encompasses a range of steps geared toward achieving communion with oneself and others
- *Hatha yoga*: the most widespread form in the West and Japan; characterized by *asanas* or poses combined in a quest for balance

How to do a Sun Salutation

The Sun Salutation is one of the most iconic exercises in hatha yoga. To do it, you simply have to follow these twelve basic movements:

1. With your feet together, stand up straight but keep your muscles relaxed. Exhale.

2. Place the palms of your hands together in front of your chest; from this position, inhale as you raise your arms above your head and bend backward slightly.

3. Exhale as you bend forward until you touch the ground with the palms of your hands, without bending your knees.

4. Stretch one leg back to touch the floor with the tips of your toes. Inhale.

5. Bring the other leg back, keeping your legs and arms straight, as you hold your breath.

6. As you exhale, bend your arms and bring your chest to the ground and then forward, resting your knees on the ground.

7. Straighten your arms and bend your spine back, keeping the lower half of your body on the ground. Inhale.

8. With your hands and feet on the ground, lift your hips until your arms and legs are straight and your body forms an upside-down V. Exhale throughout the movement.

9. Bring forward the same leg you'd stretched back earlier and bend it so that your knee and foot are aligned under your head and between your hands. Inhale.

10. Exhale as you bring your back foot forward and straighten your legs, keeping your hands on the ground as in posture 3.

11. Bring your arms above your head with your palms together and bend backward slightly, as you did in posture 2, while you inhale.

12. Lower your arms to their initial position in mountain pose while you exhale.

You've just greeted the sun; now you're ready to have a fantastic day.

Tai chi

Also known as t'ai chi ch'uan (or taijiquan), tai chi is a Chinese martial art that can be traced back hundreds of years to Buddhism and Confucianism; it is very popular in Japan, too.

According to Chinese tradition, it was created by the Taoist master and martial arts practitioner Zhang Sanfeng, though it was Yang Luchan who in the nineteenth century brought the form to the rest of the world.

Tai chi was originally a *neijia*, or internal martial art, meaning its goal was personal growth. Focused on self-defense, it teaches those who practice it to defeat their adversaries by using the least amount of force possible and by relying on agility.

Tai chi, which was also seen as a means of healing body and mind, would go on to be used more frequently to foster health and inner peace. To encourage its citizens to be more active, the Chinese government promoted it as an exercise, and it lost its original connection to martial arts, becoming instead a source of health and well-being accessible to all.

Styles of tai chi

There are different schools and styles of tai chi. The following are the best known:

- *Chen-style*: alternates between slow movements and explosive ones
- *Yang-style*: the most widespread of the forms; characterized by slow, fluid movements
- *Wu-style*: utilizes small, slow, deliberate movements
- *Hao-style*: centered on internal movements, with almost microscopic external movements; one of the least practiced forms of tai chi, even in China

Despite their differences, these styles all have the same objectives:

1. To control movement through stillness
2. To overcome force through finesse
3. To move second and arrive first
4. To know yourself and your opponent

The ten basic principles of tai chi

According to the master Yang Chengfu, the correct practice of tai chi follows ten basic principles:

1. Elevate the crown of your head, and focus all your energy there.
2. Tighten your chest and expand your back to lighten your lower body.

3. Relax your waist and let it guide your body.
4. Learn to differentiate between heaviness and lightness, knowing how your weight is distributed.
5. Relax the shoulders to allow free movement of the arms and promote the flow of energy.
6. Value the agility of the mind over the strength of the body.
7. Unify the upper and lower body so they act in concert.
8. Unify the internal and the external to synchronize mind, body, and breath.
9. Do not break the flow of your movement; maintain fluidity and harmony.
10. Look for stillness in movement. An active body leads to a calm mind.

Imitating clouds

One of the best-known movements in tai chi consists of following the form of clouds in an exercise called Wave Hands Like Clouds. Here are the steps:

1. Extend your arms in front of you with your palms down.
2. Turn your palms to face in, as though you were hugging a tree trunk.
3. Open your arms out to the side.
4. Bring the left arm up and center, and the right arm down and center.

5. Trace the shape of a ball in front of your body.
6. Turn your left palm toward your face.
7. Shift your weight to your left foot and pivot from your hip toward that side, while your eyes follow the movement of your hand.
8. Bring your left hand to your waist and your right hand in front of your face.
9. Shift your weight to your right foot.
10. Pivot toward your right, looking at your raised right hand the entire time.
11. Repeat this movement fluidly, shifting your weight from one foot to the other as you reposition your hands.
12. Stretch your arms out in front of you again and bring them down slowly, returning to your initial position.

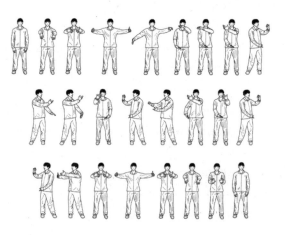

Qigong

Also known as chi kung, its name combines *qi* (life force, or energy) and *gong* (work), indicating that the form works with the individual's life force. Though relatively modern, especially under its current name, the art of qigong is based on the Tao yin, an ancient art meant to foster mental and physical well-being.

The practice began to appear in reports on training and martial arts at the beginning of the twentieth century, and by the 1930s was being used in hospitals. The Chinese government later popularized it, as it had done with tai chi.

Qigong involves static and dynamic physical exercises that stimulate respiration in a standing, seated, or reclined position. There are many different styles of qigong, but all of them seek to strengthen and regenerate *qi*. Though its movements are typically gentle, the practice is intense.

Benefits of qigong

According to numerous international scientific studies, qigong—like tai chi and yoga—offers significant health benefits. The following stand out among those proven through scientific research, as observed by Dr. Kenneth M. Sancier of San Francisco's Qigong Institute in his article "Medical Applications of Qigong"[3]:

- Modification of brain waves
- Improved balance of sex hormones
- Lower mortality rate from heart attacks
- Lower blood pressure in patients with hypertension
- Greater bone density
- Better circulation
- Deceleration of symptoms associated with senility
- Greater balance and efficiency of bodily functions
- Increased blood flow to the brain and greater mind-body connection
- Improved cardiac function
- Reduction in the secondary effects of cancer treatments

Practicing these arts not only keeps us in shape, it also helps extend our lives.

Methods for practicing qigong

In order to practice qigong correctly, we should remember that our life energy flows through our whole body. We should know how to regulate its many parts:

1. *Tyau Shenn*: (regulating the body) by adopting the correct posture—it is important to be firmly rooted to the ground

2. *Tyau Shyi*: (regulating the breath) until it is calm, steady, and peaceful

3. *Tyau Hsin*: (regulating the mind); the most complicated part, as it implies emptying the mind of thoughts

4. *Tyau Chi*: (regulating the life force) through the regulation of the three prior elements, so that it flows naturally

5. *Tyau Shen*: (regulating the spirit); the spirit is both strength and root in battle, as Yang Jwing-Ming explains in *The Essence of Taiji Qigong*.[4]

In this way, the whole organism will be prepared to work together toward a single goal.

The five elements of qigong

One of qigong's best-known exercises is a series representing the five elements: earth, water, wood, metal, and fire. This series of movements seeks to balance the five currents of energy in order to improve brain and organ function.

There are several ways to do these movements. In this case, we're following the model of Professor María Isabel García Monreal from the Qigong Institute in Barcelona.

EARTH

1. Stand with your legs apart and your feet directly below your shoulders.

2. Turn your feet outward slightly to strengthen the posture.

3. Keep your shoulders relaxed and down and your arms loose at your sides, slightly away from your body (this is the Wu Qi, or rooted, posture).

4. As you inhale, raise your arms in front of you until your hands are level with your shoulders, your palms facing down.

5. Exhale as you bend your knees and bring your arms down until your hands are level with your stomach, your palms facing in.

6. Hold this position for a few seconds, focusing on your breath.

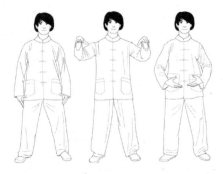

WATER

1. Starting from Earth posture, bend your knees into a squat, keeping your chest upright and exhaling throughout.
2. Press your coccyx downward to stretch your lumbar spine.
3. As you inhale, stand to return to Earth posture.
4. Repeat twice, for a total of three.

WOOD

1. Starting from Earth posture, turn your palms upward and open your arms to the side, forming a circle as you inhale, until your hands are level with your clavicle. Turn your hands so that your palms and elbows point downward, while keeping your shoulders relaxed.

2. Reverse the movement as you exhale, making a downward circle with your arms until you reach your initial position.

3. Repeat twice, for a total of three.

METAL

1. Starting from Earth posture, raise your arms until your hands are level with your sternum.
2. Turn your palms toward each other, about four inches apart, with your fingers relaxed and slightly separated, pointing upward.
3 As you inhale, move your hands away from each other until they are shoulder width apart.
4. As you exhale, bring your hands toward each other until they are back in position 2.
5. Repeat twice, for a total of three, observing the concentration of energy as you bring your hands together in front of your lungs.

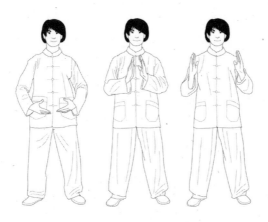

FIRE

1. Starting from Earth posture, bring your hands level with your heart as you inhale, with one hand slightly above the other and your palms facing each other.
2. Rotate your hands to feel the energy of your heart.
3. Turn from your waist gently to the left, keeping your torso relaxed and your forearms parallel to the ground.
4. With your palms still facing each other, separate your hands, bringing one up until it is level with your shoulder, and the other down in front of your abdomen.
5. Turn from your waist gently to the right, keeping your torso relaxed and your forearms parallel to the ground.
6. As you exhale, let your hands come back together in front of your heart.
7. With your palms still facing each other, separate your hands, bringing one up until it is level with your shoulder, and the other down in front of your abdomen.

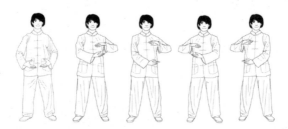

COMPLETING THE SERIES

1. Starting from Earth posture, inhale as you bring your hands level with your shoulders, palms facing down.
2. As you exhale, lower your arms to rest at your sides, returning to the initial Wu Qi posture.

Shiatsu

Created in Japan in the early twentieth century, principally for the treatment of arthritis, shiatsu also works on energy flow through the application of pressure with the thumbs and the palms of the hands. In combination with stretching and breathing exercises, it seeks to create equilibrium among the different elements of the body.

It is not important that a Tao Yin* have a name, is imitating something, or is engraved in jade. What is important is the technique and the essence of what is really practiced. Stretching and contracting, bending and lifting of the head, stepping, lying down, resting or standing, walking or stepping slowly, screaming or breathing—everything can be a Tao Yin.

—Ge Hong[5]

---

* *Tao Yin*: general term referring to the ancient arts meant to foster mental and physical well-being. http://www.gutenberg.org/ebooks/authors/search/?query=Ge,+Hong.

Breathe better, live longer

The book *Xiuzhen shishu*, known in the West as *Ten Books on the Cultivation of Perfection*, dates back to the thirteenth century and is a compendium of materials from diverse sources on developing the mind and body.

It quotes, among others, the celebrated Chinese doctor and essayist Sun Simiao, who lived during the sixth century. Sun Simiao was a proponent of a technique called the Six Healing Sounds, which involves the coordination of movement, breathing, and pronouncing sounds with the purpose of bringing our souls to a place of calm.

The six sounds are:

Xu, pronounced like "shh" with a deep sigh, which is associated with the liver

He, pronounced like "her" with a yawn, which is associated with the heart

Si, pronounced like "sir" with a slow exhale, which is associated with the lungs

Chui, pronounced like "chwee" with a forceful exhale, which is associated with the kidneys

Hoo, pronounced like "who," which is associated with the spleen

Xi, pronounced like "she," which connects the whole body

The following poem by Sun Simiao offers clues about how to live well according to the season. It reminds us of the importance of breathing, and suggests that as we breathe, we visualize the organs associated with each of the healing sounds.

In spring, breathe xu *for clear eyes and*
  so wood can aid your liver.
In summer, reach for he, *so that heart and fire can be at*
  peace.
In fall, breathe si *to stabilize and gather metal, keeping the*
  lungs moist.
For the kidneys, next, breathe chui *and see your inner waters*
  calm.
The Triple Heater needs your xi *to expel all heat and*
  troubles.
In all four seasons, take deep breaths so your spleen can
  process food.
And, of course, avoid exhaling noisily; don't let even your
  own ears hear you.
The practice is most excellent and will help preserve your
  divine elixir.

It might feel confusing to be presented with all the Eastern traditions we have introduced in this chapter. The takeaway is that they all combine a physical exercise with an awareness of our breath. These two components—movement and breath—help us to bring our consciousness in line with our body, instead of allowing our mind to be carried away by the sea of daily worries. Most of the time, we are just not aware enough of our breathing.

RESILIENCE AND WABI-SABI

How to face life's challenges without letting stress and worry age you

What is resilience?

One thing that everyone with a clearly defined *ikigai* has in common is that they pursue their passion no matter what. They never give up, even when the cards seem stacked against them or they face one hurdle after another.

We're talking about resilience, a concept that has become influential among psychologists.

But resilience isn't just the ability to persevere. As we'll see in this chapter, it is also an outlook we can cultivate to stay focused on the important things in life rather than what is most urgent, and to keep ourselves from being carried away by negative emotions.

In the final section of the chapter, we'll explore techniques that go beyond resilience to cultivate *antifragility*.

Sooner or later, we all have to face difficult moments, and the way we do this can make a huge difference to our quality of life. Proper training for our mind, body, and emotional resilience is essential for confronting life's ups and downs.

Nana korobi ya oki 七転び八起き
Fall seven times, rise eight.

—Japanese proverb

Resilience is our ability to deal with setbacks. The more resilient we are, the easier it will be to pick ourselves up and get back to what gives meaning to our lives.

Resilient people know how to stay focused on their objectives, on what matters, without giving in to discouragement. Their flexibility is the source of their strength: They know how to adapt to change and to reversals of fortune. They concentrate on the things they can control and don't worry about those they can't.

In the words of the famous Serenity Prayer by Reinhold Niebuhr:

> *God, give us grace to accept with serenity*
> *the things that cannot be changed,*
> *Courage to change the things*
> *which should be changed,*
> *and the Wisdom to distinguish*
> *the one from the other.*

Emotional resilience through Buddhism and Stoicism

Siddhārtha Gautama (Buddha) was born a prince of Kapila-vastu, Nepal, and grew up in a palace, surrounded by riches. At sixteen he married and had a child.

Not satisfied by his family's wealth, at twenty-nine he decided to try a different lifestyle and ran away from the palace to live as an ascetic. But it wasn't asceticism that he was looking for; it didn't offer the happiness and well-being he sought. Neither wealth nor extreme asceticism worked for him. He realized that a wise person should not ignore life's pleasures. A wise person can live with these pleasures but should always remain conscious of how easy it is to be enslaved by them.

Zeno of Citium began his studies with the Cynics. The Cynics also led ascetic lives, leaving behind all earthly pleasures. They lived in the street, and the only thing they owned was the clothing on their backs.

Seeing that Cynicism did not give him a sense of well-being, Zeno abandoned its teachings to found the school of Stoicism, which centers on the idea that there is nothing wrong with enjoying life's pleasures as long as they do not take control of your life as you enjoy them. You have to be prepared for those pleasures to disappear.

The goal is not to eliminate all feelings and pleasures from our lives, as in Cynicism, but to eliminate negative emotions.

Since their inception, one of the objectives of both Buddhism and Stoicism has been to control pleasure, emotions, and desires. Though the philosophies are very different, both aim to curb our ego and control our negative emotions.

Both Stoicism and Buddhism are, at their roots, methods for practicing well-being.

According to Stoicism, our pleasures and desires are not the problem. We can enjoy them as long as they don't take control of us. The Stoics viewed those who were able to control their emotions as virtuous.

What's the worst thing that could happen?

We finally land our dream job, but after a little while we are already hunting for a better one. We win the lottery and buy a nice car but then decide we can't live without a sailboat. We finally win the heart of the man or woman we've been pining for and suddenly find we have a wandering eye.

People can be insatiable.

The Stoics believed that these kinds of desires and ambitions are not worth pursuing. The objective of the virtuous person is to reach a state of tranquility (*apatheia*): the absence of negative feelings such as anxiety, fear, shame, vanity, and anger, and the presence of positive feelings such as happiness, love, serenity, and gratitude.

In order to keep their minds virtuous, the Stoics practiced something like negative visualization: They imagined the worst thing that could happen in order to be prepared if certain privileges and pleasures were taken from them.

To practice negative visualization, we have to reflect on negative events, but without worrying about them.

Seneca, one of the richest men in ancient Rome, lived a life of luxury but was, nonetheless, an active Stoic. He recommended practicing negative visualization every night before falling asleep. In fact, he not only imagined these negative situations, he actually put them into practice—for example, by living for a week without servants, or the food and drink he was used to as a wealthy man. As a result, he was able to answer the question "What's the worst thing that could happen?"

Meditating for healthier emotions

In addition to negative visualization and not giving in to negative emotions, another central tenet of Stoicism is *knowing what we can control and what we can't*, as we see in the Serenity Prayer.

Worrying about things that are beyond our control accomplishes nothing. We should have a clear sense of what we can change and what we can't, which in turn will allow us to resist giving in to negative emotions.

In the words of Epictetus, "It's not what happens to you, but how you react that matters."[1]

In Zen Buddhism, meditation is a way to become aware of

our desires and emotions and thereby free ourselves from them. It is not simply a question of keeping the mind free of thoughts but instead involves observing our thoughts and emotions as they appear, without getting carried away by them. In this way, we train our minds not to get swept up in anger, jealousy, or resentment.

One of the most commonly used mantras in Buddhism focuses on controlling negative emotions: "Oṃ maṇi padme hūṃ," in which *oṃ* is the generosity that purifies the ego, *ma* is the ethics that purifies jealousy, *ṇi* is the patience that purifies passion and desire, *pad* is the precision that purifies bias, *me* is the surrender that purifies greed, and *hūṃ* is the wisdom that purifies hatred.

The here and now, and the impermanence of things

Another key to cultivating resilience is knowing in which time to live. Both Buddhism and Stoicism remind us that the present is all that exists, and it is the only thing we can control. Instead of worrying about the past or the future, we should appreciate things just as they are in the moment, in the now.

"The only moment in which you can be truly alive is the

present moment," observes the Buddhist monk Thich Nhat Hanh.

In addition to living in the here and now, the Stoics recommend reflecting on the impermanence of the things around us.

The Roman emperor Marcus Aurelius said that the things we love are like the leaves of a tree: They can fall at any moment with a gust of wind. He also said that changes in the world around us are not accidental but rather form part of the essence of the universe—a rather Buddhist notion, in fact.

We should never forget that everything we have and all the people we love will disappear at some point. This is something we should keep in mind, but without giving in to pessimism. Being aware of the impermanence of things does not have to make us sad; it should help us love the present moment and those who surround us.

"All things human are short-lived and perishable," Seneca tells us.[2]

The temporary, ephemeral, and impermanent nature of the world is central to every Buddhist discipline. Keeping this always in mind helps us avoid excessive pain in times of loss.

Wabi-sabi and *ichi-go ichi-e*

Wabi-sabi is a Japanese concept that shows us the beauty of the fleeting, changeable, and imperfect nature of the world around us. Instead of searching for beauty in perfection, we should look for it in things that are flawed, incomplete.

This is why the Japanese place such value, for example, on an irregular or cracked teacup. Only things that are imperfect, incomplete, and ephemeral can truly be beautiful, because only those things resemble the natural world.

A complementary Japanese concept is that of *ichi-go ichi-e*, which could be translated as "This moment exists only now and won't come again." It is heard most often in social gatherings as a reminder that each encounter—whether with friends, family, or strangers—is unique and will never be repeated, meaning that we should enjoy the moment and not lose ourselves in worries about the past or the future.

The concept is commonly used in tea ceremonies, Zen meditation, and Japanese martial arts, all of which place emphasis on being present in the moment.

In the West, we've grown accustomed to the permanence of the stone buildings and cathedrals of Europe, which sometimes gives us the sense that nothing changes, making us forget about the passage of time. Greco-Roman architecture adores symmetry, sharp lines, imposing facades, and buildings and statues of the gods that outlast the centuries.

Japanese architecture, on the other hand, doesn't try to be imposing or perfect, because it is built in the spirit of *wabi-sabi*. The tradition of making structures out of wood presupposes their impermanence and the need for future generations to rebuild them. Japanese culture accepts the fleeting nature of the human being and everything we create.

The Grand Shrine of Ise,[3] for example, has been rebuilt every twenty years for centuries. The most important thing is not to keep the *building* standing for generations, but to preserve customs and traditions—things that can withstand the passage of time better than structures made by human hands.

The key is to accept that there are certain things over which we have no control, like the passage of time and the ephemeral nature of the world around us.

Ichi-go ichi-e teaches us to focus on the present and enjoy each moment that life brings us. This is why it is so important to find and pursue our *ikigai*.

Wabi-sabi teaches us to appreciate the beauty of imperfection as an opportunity for growth.

Beyond resilience: Antifragility

As the legend goes, the first time Hercules faced the Hydra, he despaired when he discovered that cutting off one of its heads meant that two would grow back in its place. He would never be able to kill the beast if it got stronger with every wound.

As Nassim Nicholas Taleb explains in *Antifragile: Things That Gain from Disorder*,[4] we use the word *fragile* to describe people, things, and organizations that are weakened when harmed, and the words *robust* and *resilient* for things that are able to withstand harm without weakening, but we don't have a word for things that *get stronger when harmed* (up to a point).

To refer to the kind of power possessed by the Hydra of Lerna, to talk about things that get stronger when they are harmed, Taleb proposes the term *antifragile*: "Antifragility is beyond resilience or robustness. The resilient resists shocks and stays the same; the antifragile gets better."

Catastrophes and exceptional circumstances offer good models for explaining antifragility. In 2011 a tsunami hit the Tōhoku region of Japan, doing tremendous damage to dozens of cities and towns along the coast, most famously Fukushima.

When we visited the affected coast two years after the

catastrophe, having driven for hours along cracked highways and past one empty gas station after another, we passed through several ghost towns whose streets had been taken over by the remnants of houses, piles of cars, and empty train stations. These towns were *fragile* spaces that had been forgotten by the government and could not recover on their own.

Other places, such as Ishinomaki and Kesennuma, suffered extensive damage but were rebuilt within a few years, thanks to the efforts of many. Ishinomaki and Kesennuma showed how *resilient* they were in their ability to return to normal after the catastrophe.

The earthquake that caused the tsunami also affected the Fukushima nuclear power plant. The Tokyo Electric Power Company engineers working at the plant were not prepared to recover from that kind of damage. The Fukushima nuclear facility is still in a state of emergency and will be for decades to come. It demonstrated its *fragility* in the face of an unprecedented catastrophe.

The Japanese financial markets closed minutes after the earthquake. Which businesses did the best in the aftermath? Stock in big construction companies has been steadily on the rise since 2011; the need to rebuild the entire coast of Tōhoku is a boon for construction. In this case, Japanese construction companies are *antifragile*, since they benefited enormously from the catastrophe.

Now let's take a look at how we can apply this concept to our daily lives. How can we be more antifragile?

Step 1: Create more options

Instead of having a single salary, try to find a way to make money from your hobbies, at other jobs, or by starting your own business. If you have only one salary, you might be left with nothing should your employer run into trouble, leaving you in a position of *fragility*. On the other hand, if you have several options and you lose your primary job, it might just happen that you end up dedicating more time to your secondary job, and maybe even make more money at it. You would have beaten that stroke of bad luck and would be, in that case, *antifragile*.

One hundred percent of the seniors we interviewed in Ogimi had a primary and a secondary occupation. Most of them kept a vegetable garden as a secondary job, and sold their produce at the local market.

The same idea goes for friendships and personal interests. It's just a matter, as the saying goes, of not putting all your eggs in one basket.

In the sphere of romantic relationships, there are those who focus all their energy on their partner and make him or her their whole world. Those people lose everything if the relationship doesn't work out, whereas if they've cultivated strong friendships and a full life along the way, they'll be in a better position to move on at the end of a relationship. They'll be anti-fragile.

Right now you might be thinking, "I don't need more than one salary, and I'm happy with the friends I've always had. Why should I add anything new?" It might seem like a waste of time to add variation to our lives, because extraordinary things don't ordinarily happen. We slip into a comfort zone. But the unexpected always happens, sooner or later.

Step 2: Bet conservatively in certain areas and take many small risks in others

The world of finance turns out to be very useful in explaining this concept. If you have $10,000 saved up, you might put $9,000 of that into an index fund or fixed-term deposit, and invest the remaining $1,000 in ten start-ups with huge growth potential—say, $100 in each.

One possible scenario is that three of the companies fail (you lose $300), the value of three other companies goes down (you lose another $100 or $200), the value of three goes up (you make $100 or $200), and the value of one of the start-ups increases twenty-fold (you make nearly $2,000, or maybe even more).

You still make money, even if three of the businesses go completely belly-up. You've benefited from the damage, just like the Hydra.

The key to becoming antifragile is taking on small risks that might lead to great reward, without exposing ourselves to dangers that might sink us, such as investing $10,000 in a fund of questionable reputation that we saw advertised in the newspaper.

Step 3: Get rid of the things that make you fragile

We're taking the negative route for this exercise. Ask yourself: What makes me fragile? Certain people, things, and habits generate losses for us and make us vulnerable. Who and what are they?

When we make our New Year's resolutions, we tend to emphasize adding new challenges to our lives. It's great to have this kind of objective, but setting "good riddance" goals can have an even bigger impact. For example:

- Stop snacking between meals
- Eat sweets only once a week
- Gradually pay off all debt
- Avoid spending time with toxic people
- Avoid spending time doing things we don't enjoy, simply because we feel obligated to do them
- Spend no more than twenty minutes on Facebook per day

To build resilience into our lives, we shouldn't fear adversity, because each setback is an opportunity for growth. If we adopt an antifragile attitude, we'll find a way to get stronger with every blow, refining our lifestyle and staying focused on our *ikigai*.

Taking a hit or two can be viewed as either a misfortune or an experience that we can apply to all areas of our lives, as we continually make corrections and set new and better goals. As Taleb writes in *Antifragile*, "We need randomness, mess, adventures, uncertainty, self-discovery, hear traumatic episodes, all these things that make life worth living." We encourage those interested in the concept of antifragility to read Nassim Nicholas Taleb's *Antifragile*.

Life is pure imperfection, as the philosophy of *wabi-sabi* teaches us, and the passage of time shows us that everything is fleeting, but if you have a clear sense of your *ikigai*, each moment will hold so many possibilities that it will seem almost like an eternity.

Ikigai: The art of living

Mitsuo Aida was one of the most important calligraphers and haikuists of the twentieth century. He is yet another example of a Japanese person who dedicated his life to a very specific *ikigai*: communicating emotions with seventeen-syllable poems, using a *shodo* calligraphy brush.

Many of Aida's haikus philosophize about the importance of the present moment, and the passage of time. The poem reproduced below could be translated as "In the here and now, the only thing in my life is your life."

いまここにしかないわたし
のいのちあなたのいのち

In another poem, Aida writes simply, "Here, now." It is an artwork that seeks to evoke feelings of *mono no aware* (a melancholy appreciation of the ephemeral).

いまここ

The following poem touches on one of the secrets of bringing *ikigai* into our lives: "Happiness is always determined by your heart."

しあわせはいつも自分の心がきめる

This last one, also by Aida, means "Keep going; don't change your path."

そのままでいいがな

Once you discover your *ikigai*, pursuing it and nurturing it every day will bring meaning to your life. The moment your life has this purpose, you will achieve a happy state of flow in all you do, like the calligrapher at his canvas or the chef who, after half a century, still prepares sushi for his patrons with love.

Conclusion

Our *ikigai* is different for all of us, but one thing we have in common is that we are all searching for meaning. When we spend our days feeling connected to what is meaningful to us, we live more fully; when we lose the connection, we feel despair.

Modern life estranges us more and more from our true nature, making it very easy for us to lead lives lacking in meaning. Powerful forces and incentives (money, power, attention, success) distract us on a daily basis; don't let them take over your life.

Our intuition and curiosity are very powerful internal compasses to help us connect with our *ikigai*. Follow those things you enjoy, and get away from or change those you dislike. Be led by your curiosity, and keep busy by doing things that fill you with meaning and happiness. It doesn't need to be a big thing: we might find meaning in being good parents or in helping our neighbors.

There is no perfect strategy to connecting with our *ikigai*. But what we learned from the Okinawans is that we should not worry too much about finding it.

Life is not a problem to be solved. Just remember to have something that keeps you busy doing what you love while being surrounded by the people who love you.

The ten rules of *ikigai*

We'll conclude this journey with ten rules we've distilled from the wisdom of the long-living residents of Ogimi:

1. **Stay active; don't retire.** Those who give up the things they love doing and do well lose their purpose in life. That's why it's so important to keep doing things of value, making progress, bringing beauty or utility to others, helping out, and shaping the world around you, even after your "official" professional activity has ended.

2. Take it slow. Being in a hurry is inversely proportional to quality of life. As the old saying goes, "Walk slowly and you'll go far." When we leave urgency behind, life and time take on new meaning.

3. Don't fill your stomach. Less is more when it comes to eating for long life, too. According to the 80 percent rule, in order to stay healthier longer, we should eat a little less than our hunger demands instead of stuffing ourselves.

4. Surround yourself with good friends. Friends are the best medicine, there for confiding worries over a good chat, sharing stories that brighten your day, getting advice, having fun, dreaming . . . in other words, living.

5. Get in shape for your next birthday. Water moves; it is at its best when it flows fresh and doesn't stagnate. The body you move through life in needs a bit of daily maintenance to keep it running for a long time. Plus, exercise releases hormones that make us feel happy.

6. Smile. A cheerful attitude is not only relaxing—it also helps make friends. It's good to recognize the things that aren't so great, but we should never forget what a privilege it is to be in the here and now in a world so full of possibilities.

7. Reconnect with nature. Though most people live in cities these days, human beings are made to be part of the natural world. We should return to it often to recharge our batteries.

8. Give thanks. To your ancestors, to nature, which provides you with the air you breathe and the food you eat, to your friends and family, to everything that brightens your days and makes you feel lucky to be alive. Spend a moment every day giving thanks, and you'll watch your stockpile of happiness grow.

9. Live in the moment. Stop regretting the past and fearing the future. Today is all you have. Make the most of it. Make it worth remembering.

10. Follow your *ikigai*. There is a passion inside you, a unique talent that gives meaning to your days and drives you to share the best of yourself until the very end. If you don't know what your *ikigai* is yet, as Viktor Frankl says, your mission is to discover it.

The authors of this book wish you a long, happy, and purposeful life.

Thank you for joining us,

HÉCTOR GARCÍA AND FRANCESC MIRALLES

NOTES

Chapter I. *Ikigai*

1   Dan Buettner. *The Blue Zones: Lessons for Living Longer from the People Who've Lived the Longest*. People in all Blue Zones (except Adventists) drink alcohol moderately and regularly. Moderate drinkers outlive nondrinkers. The trick is to drink 1–2 glasses per day (preferably Sardinian Cannonau wine), with friends and/or with food. And no, you can't save up all week and have 14 drinks on Saturday. Retrieved via https://www.bluezones.com/2016/11/power-9/#sthash.4LTc0NED.dpuf.

Chapter II. Antiaging Secrets

1   Eduard Punset. Interview with Shlomo Breznitz for *Redes*, RTVE (Radio Televisión Española). Retrieved via http://www.rtve.es/television/20101024/pon-forma-tu-cerebro/364676.shtml.

2   Howard S. Friedman and Leslie R. Martin. *The Longevity Project: Surprising Discoveries for Health and Long Life from the Landmark Eight-Decade Study.* Retrieved via http://www.penguin randomhouse.com/books/307681/the-longevity-project-by -howard-s-friedman/9780452297708/.

Chapter III. From Logotherapy to *Ikigai*

1   Viktor E. Frankl, Richard Winston (translator), Clara Winston. *The Doctor and the Soul: From Psychotherapy to Logotherapy.* Vintage, 1986.

2   Viktor E. Frankl. *Man's Search for Ultimate Meaning.* Basic Books, 2000.

3   Ibid.

4   Viktor E. Frankl. *The Will to Meaning: Foundations and Applications of Logotherapy.* Meridian/Plume, 1988.

5   Shoma Morita. *Morita Therapy and the True Nature of Anxiety-Based Disorders.* State University of New York Press, 1998.

6   Thich Nhat Hanh. *The Miracle of Mindfulness: An Introduction to the Practice of Meditation.* Beacon Press, 1996.

7   Morita. *Morita Therapy.*

Chapter IV. Find Flow in Everything You Do

1   "Crafting Fun User Experiences: A Method to Facilitate Flow— A Conversation with Owen Schaffer." Retrieved via human factors.com/whitepapers/crafting_fun_ux.asp.

2   Ernest Hemingway. *On Writing.* Scribner, 1984.

3   Bertrand Russell. *Unpopular Essays.* Routledge, 2009.

4   *The Collected Papers of Albert Einstein,* vol. 1. Princeton Univer-
     sity Press, 1987.

5   Eyal Ophir, Clifford Nass, and Anthony D. Wagner, "Cognitive
     Control in Media Multitaskers." Retrieved via www.pnas.org/
     content/106/37/15583.full.

6   Sara Thomée, Annika Härenstam, and Mats Hagberg, "Mobile
     Phone Use and Stress, Sleep Disturbances, and Symptoms of
     Depression Among Young Adults—A Prospective Cohort Study."
     Retrieved via https://www.ncbi.nlm.nih.gov/pmc/articles/PMC
     3042390/.

7   Nobuyuki Hayashi. *Idainaru Kurieteabu Derekuta No Kiseki.*
     [Steve Jobs: The Greatest Creative Director] ASCII Media
     Works, 2007. It has not been translated into English.

8   Richard P. Feynman. *"What Do You Care What Other People
     Think?": Further Adventures of a Curious Character.* W. W. Norton,
     2001.

Chapter V. Masters of Longevity

1   Emma Innes, "The secret to a long life? Sushi and sleep, accord-
     ing to the world's oldest woman," *Daily Mail.* Retrieved via
     http://www.dailymail.co.uk/health/article-2572316/The-secret
     -long-life-Sushi-sleep-according-worlds-oldest-woman.html.

2   "Muere a los 116 la mujer mas longeva según el Libro Guinness
     de los Récords," *El País.* Retrieved via http://elpais.com/elpais/
     2006/08/28/actualidad/1156747730_850215.html.

3   *Supercentenarians.* Editors: H. Maier, J. Gampe, B. Jeune, J. W.
     Vaupel, J.-M. Robine. Springer-Verlag, 2010.

4   David Batty, "World's oldest man dies at 114," *The Guardian*. Retrieved via https://www.theguardian.com/world/2011/apr/15/world-oldest-man-dies-at-114.

5   Ralph Blumenthal, "World's Oldest Man, Though Only Briefly, Dies at 111 in New York," *New York Times*. Retrieved via https://www.nytimes.com/2014/06/09/nyregion/worlds-oldest-man-though-only-briefly-dies-at-111-in-new-york.html?.

6   Henry D. Smith. *Hokusai: One Hundred Views of Mt. Fuji*. George Braziller, Inc., 1988.

7   "Old Masters at the Top of Their Game," *New York Times Magazine*. Retrieved via http://www.nytimes.com/interactive/2014/10/23/magazine/old-masters-at-top-of-their-game.html?_r=0.

8   Ibid.

9   Toshio Ban. *The Osamu Tezuka Story: A Life in Manga and Anime*. Stone Bridge Press, 2016.

10 Rosamund C. Barnett and Caryl Rivers. *The Age of Longevity: Re-Imagining Tomorrow for Our New Long Lives*. Rowman & Littlefield Publishers, 2016.

11 "Old Masters at the Top of Their Game," *New York Times Magazine*.

12 Ibid.

13 Ibid.

14 Ibid.

15 Ibid.

Chapter VI. Lessons from Japan's Centenarians

1   Strictly speaking, Shinto means "the way of the kami." In Japanese, *kami* refers to spirits or phenomena that coexist with us in nature.

2   Washington Burnap. *The Sphere and Duties of Woman: A Course of Lectures* (1848). Retrieved via https://archive-org/details/spher edutiesofwo00burn.

Chapter VII. The *Ikigai* Diet

1   Bradley J. Willcox, D. Craig Willcox, and Makoto Suzuki. *The Okinawa Program: How the World's Longest-Lived People Achieve Everlasting Health—and How You Can Too.* Retrieved via http://www.penguinrandomhouse.com/books/190921/the -okinawa-program-by-bradley-j-willcox-md-d-craig-willcox -phd-makoto-suzuki-md-foreword-by-andrew-weil-md/.

2   Luigi Fontana, Edward P. Weiss, Dennis T. Villareal, Samuel Klein, and John O. Holloszy. "Long-term Effects of Calorie or Protein Restriction on Serum IGF-1 and IGFBP-3 Concentration in Humans." Retrieved via https://www.ncbi.nlm.nih.gov/pmc/ articles/PMC2673798/.

3   Edda Cava and Luigi Fontana. "Will Calorie Restriction Work in Humans?" Retrieved via https://www.ncbi.nlm.nih.gov/ pmc/articles/PMC3765579/.

4   W. E. Bronner and G. R. Beecher. "Method for Determining the Content of Catechins in Tea Infusions by High-Performance Liquid Chromatography." Retrieved via https://www.ncbi.nlm .nih.gov/pubmed/9618918.

Chapter VIII. Gentle Movements, Longer Life

1   "Sitting Is the New Smoking," *Start Standing.* Retrieved via http://www.startstanding.org/sitting-new-smoking/.

2   Brigid Schulte, "Health Experts Have Figured Out How Much Time You Should Sit Each Day," *Washington Post*. Retrieved via https://www.washingtonpost.com/news/wonk/wp/2015/06/02/medical-researchers-have-figured-out-how-much-time-is-okay-to-spend-sitting-each-day/?utm_term=.d9d8df01a807.

3   Kenneth M. Sancier, PhD, "Medical Applications of Qigong," *Alternative Therapies*, January 1996(vol. 2, no. 1). Retrieved via http://www.ichikung.com/pdf/MedicalApplicationsQigong.pdf.

4   Yang Jwing-Ming. *The Essence of Taiji Qigong*. YMAA Publication Center, 1998.

5   Ge Hong (AD 284–364). Retrieved via https://en.wikipedia.org/wiki/Ge_Hong.

Chapter IX. Resilience and *Wabi-sabi*

1   Epictetus. *Discourses and Selected Writings*. Penguin, 2008.

2   Seneca. *Letters from a Stoic*. Penguin, 2015.

3   "Ise Shrine," *Encyclopaedia Britannica*. Retrieved via https://www.britannica.com/topic/Ise-Shrine.

4   Nassim Nicholas Taleb. *Antifragile: Things That Gain from Disorder*. Random House, 2014.

SUGGESTIONS FOR FURTHER READING

The authors of *Ikigai* were greatly inspired by:

Breznitz, Shlomo, and Collins Hemingway. *Maximum Brain-power: Challenging the Brain for Health and Wisdom*. Ballantine Books, 2012.

Buettner, Dan. *The Blue Zones: Lessons for Living Longer from the People Who've Lived the Longest*. Retrieved via http://www.bluezones.com/2016/11/power-9/#sthash.4LTc0NED.dpuf.

Csikszentmihalyi, Mihaly. *Flow: The Psychology of Optimal Experience*. Harper Perennial, 1990.

Frankl, Viktor E. *The Doctor and the Soul: From Psychotherapy to Logotherapy*. Vintage, 1986.

———. *Man's Search for Ultimate Meaning*. Basic Books, 2000.

———. *The Will to Meaning: Foundations and Applications of Logotherapy*. Meridian/Plume, 1988.

Friedman, Howard S., and Leslie R. Martin. *The Longevity Project: Surprising Discoveries for Health and Long Life from the Landmark Eight-Decade Study.* Plume, 2012.

Morita, Shoma. *Morita Therapy and the True Nature of Anxiety-Based Disorders.* State University of New York Press, 1998.

Taleb, Nassim Nicholas. Incerto series: *Fooled by Randomness, The Black Swan, The Bed of Procrustes, Antifragile.* Random House, 2012.

Willcox, Bradley J., D. Craig Willcox, and Makoto Suzuki. *The Okinawa Diet Plan: Get Leaner, Live Longer, and Never Feel Hungry.* Clarkson Potter, 2001.

Héctor García is a citizen of Japan, where he has lived for over a decade, and of Spain, where he was born. He is the author of several books about Japanese culture, including two worldwide bestsellers, *A Geek in Japan* and *Ikigai*. A former software engineer, he worked at CERN in Switzerland before moving to Japan.

Francesc Miralles is an award-winning and internationally bestselling author of books about how to live well, together with the novels *Love in Small Letters* and *Wabi-Sabi*. Alongside Héctor García, he was welcomed to Okinawa in Japan, where the inhabitants live for longer than in any other place in the world.

There they had the chance to interview more than a hundred villagers about their philosophy for a long and happy life.